S0-AXD-904

True to Life
Adventure Stories

True to Life Adventure Stories

VOLUME ONE

Judy Grahn, Editor

THE CROSSING PRESS / Trumansburg, New York 14886

The Crossing Press Feminist Series

Twenty Days Copyright © 1978 by Sharon Isabell. Used by permission of the author.
Zio Copyright © 1978 by Alma R. Vanek. Used by permission of the author.
Ruby Mae Copyright © 1978 by Nyla. Used by permission of the author.
The Light Copyright © 1978 by Linnea A. Due. Used by permission of the author.
Charm School Copyright © 1978 by Sandy Boucher. Used by permission of the author.
Steven Copyright © 1978 by Kate Inman. Used by permission of the author.
The Grandchild Copyright © 1978 by Evan Rubin. Used by permission of the author.
In Memoriam: Carolyn Johnson Copyright © 1978 by Chris Llewellyn. Used by per-
      mission of the author.
Susie Q Copyright © 1978 by Red Arobateau. Used by permission of the author.
Glass Copyright © 1978 by Judy Grahn. Used by permission of the author.
A Trip to Chicago Copyright © 1978 by Joyce Maupin. Used by permission of the author.
The Woman Fables, 1–12 Copyright © 1978 by Dell Fitzgerald Richards. Used by
      permission of the author.
The Three Bears Copyright © 1978 by Ruth Babcock. Used by permission of the author.
Puddin Copyright © 1978 by Norma Stafford. Used by permission of the author.
It's Hard to Stay Dry in the Ocean Copyright © 1978 by Helle. Used by permission of the author.
Shoes Copyright © 1978 by Pat Parker. Used by permission of the author.
Masks & Mirrors Copyright © 1978 by Nancy Green. Used by permission of the author.
THAT MESERABLE SCAR Copyright © 1978 by Linda Marie. Used by permission of the author.
Turtle Voices Copyright © 1978 by Mary Jo McConahay. Used by permission of the author.
The Last of the Weekend Visits Copyright © 1978 by Kathryn Kendall. Used by
      permission of the author.

Copyright © 1978 by Diana Press

Originally published by Diana Press, this edition (1983) is part of
The Crossing Press Feminist Series.

Library of Congress Cataloging in Publication Data

Main entry under title:

True to life adventure stories.

    1. Short stories, American--Women authors.
2. Lesbianism--Fiction. 3. Feminism--Fiction.
I. Grahn, Judy, 1940–
PZ1.T76 [PS647.W6]   813'.01   78–16251
ISBN O–88447–025–3

Contents

Murdering The King's English

I began gathering these stories together in 1974, having asked myself the question: What *is* a woman's adventure story, and getting no reply whatsoever. As the stories began coming in, with three volumes forming in my mind, I realized that the collection would be like nothing I had ever read or imagined.

As a teenager in a small town during the fifties, I spent many afternoons reading my father's men's adventure magazines, tense dramas of men alone in the mountains with a lion, and only one long range rifle, six powerful shells and a quart of Seagram Seven to knock him over with. The purposes behind knocking over the many lions, sharks, and alligators in these stories was never clear, only that this was all 'high adventure'. In the last men's magazine I remember reading, Our Hero was a fumigator trapped for the afternoon in a garage with a dozen black widow spiders. This made me howl—and begin to suspect that men's 'adventures' were a shuck, since black widow spiders lived in all our neighbors' garages and I went in them all the time.

I turned then to 'true' romance stories, gripping sagas of drive-in movie seductions, long scenes of how a family came to terms with their pregnant, unmarried daughters or other transgressors of patriarchal sexual taboos. These stories were more realistic in their situations than the men's magazines, but their conclusions were ridiculously different from the way things actually happen, and monotonously paternalistic in their moral tone.

Finally, I tried literary magazine short stories taught in literature classes. And here, I found, the point of view was almost entirely upperclass, the bias that of the few people who hire service workers and not the many who are; stories about the alienation of people with money, the problems of the professional class, with ordinary people seen from a great class distance. I found them boring, condescending, and false to living as I knew it.

Fortunately, there were some women writers who saved the day for me: Carson McCullers, Shirley Jackson, Flannery O'Connor. They wrote about all kinds of people, their women were real instead of cardboard or seen only for what they have to do with men, and they rarely used stereotypes for the sake of a dramatic point.

Then more recently the upsurge of available Black women's stories has given me a new sense of the usefulness of literature. Alice Walker's finely honed, *In Love and Trouble,* Mary Washington's tightly edited, excellent anthology, *Black-eyed Susans,* Ntozake Shange's wonderful *Sassafras,* Zora Neale Hurston's traditional, historical collection *Mules and Men.*

And now, to add to them, where are the multitudes of other American voices to speak truthfully about the tremendous variety of women's lives, and to break down the stereotypes we have all been caught in?

As the manuscripts for True to Life Adventure Stories began coming in, I realized I was picking them for their realistic grappling with real-life situations, for unsentimentality and clarity, for integrity. They are not escapist, not fantasies about winning, or leaving, or controlling the world. They do what I had hoped stories would do: Provoke, teach, reveal women to other women, arouse strong emotions, redefine—because they are true. By true I mean they are based on information which is close to, or is, the original source of the story. They begin to unveil what it is that women know, woman by woman, and from where she is standing. They do not attempt to use characters as symbols or stereotypes, and they do not try to act out a wishful thinking.

Let me give an example of what I mean by wish-fulfillment writing. D.H. Lawrence's *The Fox*, written in 1922, is a story about two lesbians who have been living on a farm and have grown tired of each other. A young man comes along, woos and marries one, and a tree conveniently falls on the other one and kills her. The tree plays a major part in the story, as a modern male symbol (Anciently, the 'tree of life' stood for *female* power).

The Fox is the most famous, most widely read and studied, most publicized, filmed and written-about lesbian story ever produced, and this is because Lawrence, as his story shows, was anti-lesbian. Consider if a woman had written *The Fox*, and had it be reversed, with a woman breaking into the tail-end of a marriage, and with a symbolic matriarchal tree falling conveniently on the head of the unwanted husband. You see what I mean about wish fulfillment and escapist fantasies passing as truth in literature.

In the prefaces for these three volumes, I want to explore three different aspects of what the stories mean to me, and what they can possibly teach us. In Volume I, I would like to focus on their language, in volume II, their 'characters', or persons, and in Volume III, their plots.

How a thing is said has everything to do with what is said. A blunt, forceful statement has more urgency than a subtle, suggestive statement. It is more aggressive, and I certainly wanted aggressive stories which were at the same time true-to-life, neither altered for the sake of drama, nor obscured for the sake of safety.

There has often been a false argument in artistic circles, about the supposed difference between content and form, arguments about which is more important: what is said, or how it is said. The real question is, how much reality can anyone stand to read about especially about women. And what will we learn from a story when the writer is saying exactly what she knows about, and when the writer is an original source of the story.

Some of the pieces in these three volumes use language in a way which is not ususally seen in print, except to make fun of it, or to quote someone. I am not talking about swearwords. I'm talking about the use of forms of working-class English which are much less acceptable in modern American literature than swearwords, class snobbery, racist and sexist portrayals of people, outright lies, etc. Worse than any of those things is to, for instance, spell a word differently than Mr. Webster, in a workingclass manner. Witness ee cummings, who drove typesetters crazy. But to express workingclass writing as workingclass people do it, that is considered: *illiterate.* Not-literate, not able to read and write, with an underlying implication that it also means not able to think.

I had no idea this was such a touchy subject until 1973 when I helped publish Sharon Isabell's autobiographical novel, *Yesterday's Lessons.* (Women's Press Collective, Diana Press). Her story, "Twenty Days", leads off this volume. In the most important typing job of my life, I did the typesetting for *Yesterday's Lessons.*

I will never again be able to spell the word clumbsy any other way except 'clumbsy', which is how Sharon spells it. Fortunately for my own education, she has not been run through the sieve of academic English; she has retained much of the language of her white workingclass family, and she writes with her own ears instead of Mr. Webster's—or mine.

We have received scathing letters and comments because I refused to standardize Isabell's English, not only her spelling, but her punctuation and syntax as well. (Arrangements of words). We were criticized for not obscuring the utter clarity of her sentences, for not rearranging the fast-paced events of her life into a smoother, falsely dramatic, more climactic style. We had been irresponsible, we were told; we were giving women a bad name, giving lesbians a bad name, giving the entire workingclass a bad name. We were not fit to call ourselves publishers. Gracious!

As a result of this class position, and of having to defend our editorial decision not to tamper with workingclass English, I have given a good deal of thought to the origins of folk English, to women and English, to the King's English, and to the phrase, 'murdering the King's English'. Murdering the King's English can be a crime only if you identify with the King.

Editors usually function as filters between people's own stories (political & social stances) and the owners of patriarchal publishing companies. Editors 'clean up' or 'uplift' a story whose common English is considered 'dirty' or low. They rifle through it looking for eccentricities, soften its anger and outrage, take away what is aggressive, what is detailed, specific, physical—and instead substitute what is abstract, distant, objective, passive.

You may notice that in *True to Life Adventures* there is never an outside and all-knowing narrator who speaks standard English while quoting characters who speak what is called 'dialect' or slang, or people's English. "I never meant to steal from no poor people," Isabell says as she is being hauled off to jail in "Twenty Days", and she is speaking as the

narrator, not quoting someone else. For anyone to have edited her sentence conventionally, by changing the the word
no to *any*, would also be saying that the occupation of writer belongs only to the upper class and those who can *pass*
by using its standards; no one else need apply—except as a
character, an object to be quoted and described, and in effect, looked down upon from a class distance.

This does not mean that I have said, "Anything goes,
everything a person writes is fine and should be printed any-
which way," for the sake of some halfbaked notion of auth-
enticity or phony democracy. The standards I have used are
geared to common English, and in particular to other-than-
academic writing, but they are still standards, still the use of
critical judgement.

I wanted precision, and in real precision the content and
form are the same, there is no contradiction between them.
It is both making actual your beliefs and taking your beliefs
from what is actual. Even those sections which are clearly-
marked fantasies are more actual than not, and illustrate
what I think are frequent female imaginings.

I also wanted variety, and that is certainly here, for many
other institutions besides colleges harbor and train writers.
The forty-five writers in these volumes have learned their
discipline, collected their ideas, practiced their craft not in
colleges only—jails too, mental hospitals too, and more fre-
quently the hidden institutions for women such as trade
schools, service jobs, office jobs, family work, street hustling.

They have likewise gathered their political ideas from
various institutions: the labor-oriented old Left, the historic
lesbian underground, the Black Liberation movement, the
Women's Liberation movement, and mostly from life in
general. So many adjectives would describe this wide range

of stories—hilarious, terrifying, revealing, harping... And throughout, the language remains intact, precise for the story it is telling, which could not be told in any other way, and be the same story.

"yes your allowed to moan and cry," Helle wrote about the job of hooking during a hot New York summer. I found this story buried in a box in her room, having been moved too many times to count, scorched, crumpled, splotched and chewed on by a dog or a child. The center of one paragraph was missing, so I left it that way, since it is easy enough for a reader to fill in the blanks.

Content and form, as Felicia Newme once said, go together—like a face. Of *course.* I do not understand 'God-in-three-persons', I cannot comprehend the 'Goddess in her three aspects', and the alleged duality of good and evil baffle me completely. But content and form, that I think I understand. They are two versions of the same. They operate equally, and harmoniously.

That is, they should do that. When they don't there is exploitation, thievery and misuse, and, as Felicia often said while reading manuscripts, 'Lies, lies, lies.'

Art, in my terms, is like a basket, and a basket is useful. The *idea* of a basket, of something constructed to carry things, is certainly useful. You could say that a basket is an idea (a form) made of straw (which is the content). Or you could say that the idea of a basket (a portable container) is the content, and the woven straw is the *form,* as an egg is another kind of form, and a clay jar is another and so on to containers (ideas) such as houses, trains, ships—and stories. A 'workingclass' story which is not told in a workingclass manner is only half a story. The more closely coordinated we allow the content and form of any writing to be, the more accurate, useful, and whole it is.

I have used a number of poems in these collections, treating them exactly as the other stories, since they contain the same amount of information. I can't think of a better example of a story told in its own language than Chris Llewellyn's poem, "In Memoriam: Carolyn Johnson" (Vol. I). Using the language of office workers—*white out, index, carriage return*—she has created a moving memorial to another secretary like herself. Doing this means taking women's work seriously, to make a poem with images which have not been considered poetic or literary, ever since the labor of secretaries switched from English 'clarks', who were men, to 'girl Fridays', who are women.

Speaking of the King's English, the term 'girl Friday' comes from Daniel Defoe, an Englishman who wrote a novel in support of English colonialism, called *Robinson Crusoe*. In it a white man is stranded on an island with only one native person, a darkskinned man the Englishman thinks of as his servant. He calls him his 'man Friday', because he found him on a Friday.

Women's art, feminist writing, has a definition which I have used in this anthology: it must be useful to women, must work in our interest. Must not work to divide us further, must not lie about us to each other, must not give false information which would fall apart when people try to make use of it.

Let us suppose that the truth is tangible, is both an idea, and a tangible, perceivable material substance. Like a bean, or a book. Anyone can fantasize a book, but to make a book, to type and print, to carry around all those tons of paper and shape them into a form which is 8 X 10 and glued together, that is a different matter. That takes the machinery, muscle, material substance which is the other side of an

idea. It is not an accident that workingclass women produced the material substance of this book, and that the stories
say what they do. So let us suppose that like a bean or a
book, truth has content and form, and that the way the truth
is told has everything to do with how true it is, how material
it is, how much material substance it has. And how useful.
And useful to who? (Note: *whom* is the standard form. But
'to-who' is prettier and sounds like an owl. It has a fuller
content).

And that is the gist of the matter, our language, like our
lives, should belong to us.

The voices of these many writers speak from where they
are standing, without tricks or larger than life amplifiers.
The result is as intimate and dramatic as outbursts at the
kitchen table. The reclamation of ideas, political directions,
culture—in which we are involved with the independent
women's presses and other institutions supported by women
make it possible for women to begin to speak honestly, and
in a whole voice; to say what we actually see and think in a
tone of voice and language which is appropriate to the
writer's life and to the lives of millions of other women. The
more we do this, the more concrete information we will all
have to realistically appraise our situations, our relationships
to each other and to the world. And the more realistically
we will act to gain control over our lives, without fantasy
and false assumption.

Twenty Days

Sharon Isabell

The Judgc was dressed in black and his face was hidden behind the paper mask of athority which he had began to believe was his heart. His supream position was known and the woman that stood before him knew she was at his mercy. The tears began to flood her eyes and she began to plead.

"Your Honer, Please don't send me to jail. I have a job. My two children. Please I'll pay back the money. I'll never do anything again. I've never been in trouble before. Please!"

"I'm going to put you on two years probation. You also must spend two weekends in the county jail. Next case."

I wanted to throw-up. The room made me sick. One man sitting in his high place, as the cattle was run before him to be branded or kicked which ever pleased him the most. The public defender sat with his hands on his head trying to figure out which file belonged to what person. It was hard for him becausc hc was defending twenty different people that he had never seen before. They really had a good defence. That was the law.

15

The hate flowed through me and I felt the strenth of it.
My fear was weak and my hate killed it. I held my head up
just like my aunt had told me to do. She told me never to
bow my head to nothing. I looked in the Judges eyes and he
blinked in surprise. I kept looking in his eyes and he became
noticeably unconfortable.

"Do you have anything to say?"

"No."

"Twenty days in the county jail. Three years probation
and restitution. Next case."

My sister had tears in her eyes and she was shaking. She
looked so out of place in that court room She looked so
poor and beaten, standing in a room of fine wood, flags and
cement. I wanted to cry when I looked at my sister. But
they took me in another room to wait for the policewoman
who would take me twenty miles to the county jail. I had to
go to the bathroom. A woman walked me to the bathroom.
I came out of the bathroom and a policewoman was knocking on the back door. I went to open the door for her and
everyone in the place jumped up and came running after
me. They thought I was trying to get away.

The policewoman handcuffed me and then took me out
to the police car. I felt like one of the ten most wanted or
something. I felt like laughing. Just laughing until I passed
out. But I didn't laugh. As we drove through town people
tried to see who I was. I felt like yelling, its ma barker in
the flesh. But I couldn't yell.

People keep turning and looking at me. I began to think
about what was written on the paper I got in court. The
people vs Sharon Isabell. I wanted to call out to the people,
I didn't hurt no poor people. I only wrote bad checks to

the rich stores that use to make fun of my mother when she went in them to buy my school close. How could I ever forget the way they treated my mother. The way they made her feel so low. My mother is the greatest woman I ever knew, or would hope to know but all my life I had to stand and watch small people mistreet her and abuse her because she was not upper class and did not dress in there cloths and speek there perfect English. If she would have had the opertunities which they had she would have been twise as good at everything and she would still have known how to treat people, *all people with respect.*

When I got to the jail they started booking me. I felt helpless against them. They made me feel like I wasn't me. They put me in a small cell. I climed up on the top bunk. I sat there and I began to turn into a different person. I began to remember when I was little and how I use to have to fight. But most of all I remembered the hate, it was so strong. They brought me a tray of food and I told them I wasn't hungry. I didn't want nothin from them. They brought another woman in the cell. She looked like she was about fifty. She kept talking about how they weren't going to keep her there. She didn't stick her boy friend. Some one else knifed him. Then they came in and told us to take off our cloths they were going to spray us. I told them to go to hell!

"Look Isabell, either you take off your cloths or I'll get one of the men Sheriff's to help me take them off."

I took off my cloths and threw them on the floor but I didn't bend over and let her spray my ass like she told me to do. No one would ever make me bend over unless they killed me. I stared at the matron with all the hate I felt. We were then taken in the main cell. As we walked in the

17

room thirty women looked us up and down. The matron told me to wait a minute. The captain wants to see you before you go in the main cell.

I was taken to this office and told to sit down. This captain came in the room and sit down and then looked at me and said:

"I received the word that your a lesbian. I want to tell you something. Twenty days in here is really hard. But if you so much as look at a woman while your here I'll put you in the hole without a blanket or cigarettes and let you stay there. Let me tell you that's the hardest time you'll ever spend in your life. Am I clear."

I just sat there and looked at the creep and didn't answer him. I knew I was going to hate this place. So I looked like a lesbian hu, so what. He looked like a bastard.

I walked in the main cell and I hated all the women in there and the way they looked at me. I hated myself for being there. Everyone hated everyone. I went over and sat in a corner. I light my last cigarette. One by one the women came over to me and ask me how long I was in for. I told them to stay away from me hadn't they heard I wasn't supose to talk to anyone. They said they never heard of such a thing.

"No one can make you not talk to anyone."

The matron came in and told us to get in our night cells. They were even smaller and eight of us were squashed together for the night. With a open toilet to keep us company and bars pulled tighter around us. I layed in a steel slab that was attached to the wall, on it I had a inch thick mattress and one sheet and two army blankets. I didn't know the woman that slep over my head or the ones all around me. We were locked up together tho. It was dark and outside the bars was air but I couldn't reach that far and I had to breath. For a minute I thought I was going to die. I was scared. —I lived, so I guess you don't have to breath to stay alive.

At 5:00 a.m. the matron told us to get up. The women walked in slow motion and no one smiled.

"I got to the fucken sink first. What the fuck you doin. When I was on the streets my old man fucked me every day."

Then we lined up for breakfast. There was a slot in the door and they pushed threw some food.

"Just look at this shit. The fuckin milk is curtled. I aint eatin none of this Fuckin oat meal with sour milk."

We sat at a picknic table in the middle of a 20 by 10 room. The other furnishings were, one sink, one toilet that had a sheet hung up in front of it, and benches scattered around. No one ate that oat meal but we all ate two pices of toast that was soggy with margine.

We all sat in the small room looking at each other wondering what we could say or do. Then two women sat next to each other and compared niddle tracks. They were both heroin addicts. Then a tall thin woman stood up and began to pace the room. She began talking but she wasn't talking to anyone.

"I think I have it figured out. I've been thinking about how to get away with credit cards. Me and my boy friend got busted but I think I've figured out a way to get away with it the next time."

"Why don't you sit down and shut your stupid mouth, you dumb bitch."

"Why don't you try and make me?"

"I'll kill your fuckin ass."

The two women started for each other and everyone started yelling at them. Look you two will get us all in trouble.

All of a sudden everyone was smiling. The matron came in and gave us lists of stuff we could buy if we had any money. Then I found out that if your in jail and don't have any money, you were in bad shape. We were only allowed to buy twenty candy bars and one carton of cigarettes. We also could buy tooth paste and stuff like that. The food was so bad that most of the women kept going on twenty candy bars a week. When they brought our stuff in the rest of the day was spent trading and bargining with everyone and the women who had no money sat like hungry animals watching and waiting for a chance to grab something.

"That fuckin bitch stole my candy bar. I'm gonna kill her. Your not supost to steal from us you no good bitch. Thats a rule we don't steal from each other. "

I felt like the bench I was sitting on. Nothing shocked or suprised me. Nothing made me feel anything. All the angry words filtered through my ears. All my life I had heard angry words. When I was a small child I learned that life was angry words. No one was shocked then either. No one held their hands over my ears. My mother tried but there were to many and she had so much to fight against.

I stood by the window a lot. Nothing seemed the same tho. I couldn't reach anything. The coffee was full of sugar to keep us fat. They served us meat one night and we all sat around the table and ate with our hands because it was to tough to eat with a fork. I felt like a animal. Everyone looked like animals. We only had spoons.

I had to go to the bathroom and while I was sitting on the toilet a woman opened the curtain. I wanted to kill her. The other women wanted to kill her. One woman had tried to kill her but I stoped her the day before. I was to angry this time.

Everyone in the room saw me sitting on the toilet. So when a woman jumped on her and started beating her I didn't stop it. I was glad she was being beat up. I didn't care if she was killed.

The matron and a male Sherriff came in. The one woman was lying on the floor and they wanted to know who else was in the fight. No one answered. No one was a snitch. They questioned all of us but no one would tell. They locked the one woman in the hole. For three days and three nights she screamed. I couldn't sleep and I wished it was me instead of her. She was dieing. The matron said she was trying to pretend she was crazy so she could get out of the hole. After the three days and nights they took her screaming like a animal to the State mental hospital.

Once a week on a Thursday we could have visitors, between 10:00 a.m. and 12:00, and between 1:00 and 3:00 p.m. All the parents wanted to look at the criminals their daughters were in jail with. Of course it was a mistake that their kids were in jail or a slip but those others, what did they do? I sat and watched the relatives stare and I wanted to laugh. I wanted to stand and laugh until I fell down. Understanding was easy when it was your own. But those others!

Zio

Alma R. Vanek

Alma hated the snow when it melted into waters that ran wild down the mountains, because it kept her friend, Zio from coming to see her. Next to Mama, she loved this man she named Zio, best in the whole world. Alma was happy when he rode down from the highest mine in Colorado. Zio had a red smiling face and hair like melted copper pennies. He always looked too big for his horse.

When Alma was small and Zio was still boss at the mine, he would swoop her into his arms, and the rough wool of his red plaid mackinaw would scratch her face. From high on his shoulder she would announce with glee, "Mama, Zio is here, Zio is here."

Mama was always busy with a houseful of boarders and the care of the baby, who was often sick; but she would stop what she was doing and welcome him with her glad smile. Big Sister would come running and Baby Brother would bang his high chair to show he was happy too, that Zio, their best friend was here.

Zio would laugh and say to Mama, "Anytime you don't want these kids, I'll take them with me."

It was Zio who helped Alma build a tree house by the fern-edged pool, where the biggest lady slippers fitted the feet of her smallest doll. He even came to Echo Rock, to listen to the funny distorted sounds, where his big laugh boomed back accented with her giggles. Zio was the only one who wanted to know what new names she had discovered and given herself, because she didn't like her own name, Alma.

"What's the new name this time?"

"Ecuador."

"Now where did you find this one?"

"In Big Sister's geography book."

"I like this best so far."

When Zio came alone he brought candy and always had time to play games and listen to Alma's adventures. But after his heart trouble, he opened a saloon, because he couldn't work in the mine anymore.

Then everything changed, and when he came down his wife, Sorina came with him. Sorina was almost as big as Zio and her hair was as jet black as the inside of a lump of coal. She never smiled and she wore black because a brother was killed in the World War that was going on in Europe.

Sorina always brought her pack of greasy fortune telling cards and laid them out for Mama. They never showed anything but bad luck. Then Sorina wanted to see Mama's Italian dream book. They would turn the brittle ragged pages carefully, and always Mama's dreams would spell disaster. Mama would be sad for days, sure that something terrible would happen.

Sorina was having bad dreams about Giorgio, a gambler who had just built a saloon, right above theirs.

"This devil Giorgio sees we're doing good business, so he sneaks around and gets The Mine to lease him the ground right above us. I tried to stop him. I knew all his slops and the water would come down on top of us. I saw trouble right away in the cards and now it's bad in the dream book."

Zio didn't like the cards or the bad dream signs and told Mama. "Cards are pieces of paper. How can they tell what is going to happen?" But Mama believed anything Sorina predicted.

Like the time Baby Brother was real sick. Sorina laid the cards and predicted. "Somebody here is going to die soon. Like I always say, we can't escape our fate." Mama began to cry. Alma stood in front of Sorina. "Why do you make Mama cry with your bad cards?" Mama slapped her.

Alma ran to her hiding place in the attic. Hours later, when Zio found her he told her he had brought the doctor and Baby Brother was feeling better. He wasn't angry with her and seemed just the same until the last time they visited.

That last time they had come down to see the doctor, because Zio was having trouble with his heart again. He didn't play games and even his smile seemed far away.

Sorina was rushing him. "You know we have to get back. I'm afraid what that devil Giorgio will do when he knows we're gone. I had a big fight with him, when he dumped his slops in our yard. He called me a witch and ordered me off his property, when I called him a devil. He's so jealous of our business, he'd do anything."

Zio interrupted. "I don't want these fights. We have to get along or it'll get worse."

"You bet it will get worse. Just wait till the snow starts to melt and water runs like crazy down the mountain and into the saloon."

"It didn't run in the saloon last year, when I made the ditch."

"Last year we made the ditch where we wanted, because that devil Giorgio wasn't on top of us. Remember this year the ditch starts on his property and he'd like to wash us right off the mountain."

"Don't worry I'll fix the ditch."

"Doctor told you. Take it easy, no more hard work."

"I'll work it out with Giorgio about the ditch. No fights."

"You can't work with that devil. I told you when he came that the cards showed bad trouble and now the dreams are worse."

"It's always the cards or the dreams with you. Let's go."

Alma was trying to tell Zio her surprise. She was right on his heels. She touched his sleeve and let the words tumble out. "I'm the only one picked in the second grade to play a part in the senior class play. I'm a pony."

Zio bent down and smiled right at her. "They were smart to pick you. You'll make a fine pony. Stand big, so you'll see me right in the front row. If you do fine, I'll treat you at the ice cream parlor. I promise."

"How do you know you can come? By then the snow will be melting and the water running wild."

"Don't worry. We'll have the ditch fixed and everything will be fine."

"You always think everything will be fine. I know there will be trouble. You better not make any promises to her."

"Don't look so sad little Pony. Remember, I promise, I'll come to see you."

Saturday morning, a week before the play, Alma woke up happy and excited. Today, was the day to pick up her new Mary Jane slippers and go to the dress rehearsal. Feet first, she jumped out of bed into a pool of sunbeams. She paused a minute to warm her toes in their rainbow fire.

After rehearsal, Miss Moran, the coach, sewed ostrich plumes on her headgear. Alma confided that Zio was coming down to see her in the play.

"All that way to see you? He must really like you."

"Oh, yes."

"He'll be proud of you. You're my best pony."

Usually Alma was bubbling over with words, but this

time she was so overwhelmed with the praise that she couldn't utter a word. She felt happy enough to fly.

All the way home Alma skipped and flapped her arms to make believe she was flying. She lighted for a second to peek into the ice cream parlor, where Zio promised he would take her after the play. She had never tasted a sundae or soda, just ice cream cones. She skipped on, savoring this delicious choice; but remembered in time not to step on the cracks in the sidewalk. Big Sister had warned her, not to break her mama's back. She would never do that, she loved Mama so, and had such important things to tell her today.

Alma burst into the kitchen shouting, "Mama, Mama."

But Mama wasn't there. Baby Brother was crying and Sister was trying to feed him. The boarders were standing like statues.

Alma began to cry too. "Where is Mama, where is Mama?"

"Mama went to help Sorina. Zio was killed dead."

Alma screamed. "Zio, Zio . . . . . Dead? No, no, not my Zio."

"Yes." Big Sister was crying too. "Zio's dead."

"Why?"

"A fight about the ditch. Giorgio cut a hole in Zio's head."

"Please I want to see my Zio. Not dead . . . Zio promised to come to see me in the Play. I told Miss Moran he was coming."

Sister was trying to quiet Baby Brother who was screaming and choking. Alma was sobbing so hard she began to shake with hiccups. "Zio, Zio . . . ."

One of the boarders took Alma into his arms. He fed her sips of diluted tamarindo and whiskey to stop her hiccups.

When Alma awoke Sunday morning she was in Mama's bed with all her clothes on. Her eyes hurt and her mouth was sawdust dry. Then she remembered.

Mama had found Sorina covered with Zio's blood. She had sat in the running ditch holding Zio in her arms, until the Sheriff came to arrest Giorgio. Sorina had refused to move until Giorgio was handcuffed and brought down to jail.

Mama brought Sorina back to stay for the funeral. She was sick with a cold.

Sorina kept repeating the story of how Giorgio had chopped a hole in Zio's head to kill him. When Sorina had gotten up Saturday morning, water was running through the saloon. Sorina ran out and began to mend the side of the ditch that had been cut. Zio had fixed the ditch on Friday and the work had hurt his heart. Sorina didn't want Zio to come now, but he came anyway. When Giorgio came out with a pickax, Sorina called him bad names and accused him of cutting the ditch. Giorgio knocked the shovel from her hands. Zio lifted his shovel to protect her and at the same instant Giorgio brought the pickax down on Zio's head.

Sorina never stopped crying and talked until her voice was a croaky whisper. Alma felt too tired to cry anymore, but around Sorina the crying never stopped.

Alma was glad Mama let her go to school Monday morning so she could tell her teacher about Zio. "I can't come to school tomorrow, because it's Zio's funeral. Could I tell Miss Moran that I can't practice today or tomorrow and that maybe I can't be in the Play."

Alma confided to Miss Moran that she didn't want to see Zio dead with the big bloody cut that Sorina kept talking about.

Miss Moran asked if she could come home to talk with Mama. Alma stayed in her room until Mama and Miss Moran had finished talking. Mama called her. "You don't have to go to the funeral. Miss Moran says it wouldn't be good for you to see Zio dead. You can still be in the Play. Miss Moran says you practice good and she needs you."

How Alma wished Zio had been there to see her when she pranced out on the stage, right down to the front. For a second when the footlights blinded her, she thought she saw Zio. She was wishing so hard. But if Zio had been there, Mama wouldn't be crying.

Then school ended.

One day Alma asked Mama, "Where is Zio now?" Mama began to cry so hard she had to sit down. Big Sister scolded Alma for making Mama cry. Alma never asked about Zio again, but when she was running through the wet meadows or scrambling up the mountain slopes she began to think-talk with Zio. She only did this when she was alone out of doors. First, she would look into the sky, where she believed he might be. To think-talk she didn't even have to move her lips. It was like saying prayers in church where she wasn't supposed to whisper or move her lips.

Alma forgot Sorina, until Sister told her she had moved from the place where Zio was killed. She was living in the Dalla house on the edge of town, across the river.

One night, Mama made them hurry with supper, because Sorina wanted them to come. Alma begged not to go. She was afraid because Sister told her that Sorina had a row of lemons in her cellar, with rusty nails stuck in them. They were for people she hated and would bring them bad luck, or make them die as the lemons rotted. "She stuck thirteen rusty nails in the lemon that's for Giorgio, who killed Zio."

Sorina's house was across the old bridge. In the daytime it was fun and scary to play on the bridge. But every child knew that the bridge was haunted at night.

In the Spring, the massive waters of the river would explode against a giant boulder to lift and catapult it against the bridge. The bridge would shake and groan as if every timber was breaking. Alma would shriek, "A giant!" and cling to the railing with all her strength. Sometimes Alma and her friends would dare to close their eyes and pretend they were riding a great ship to the end of the river. But when the river was in flood, a momentous force of roiling waters would sledgehammer the banks, clawing out rocks and pulling down trees, as a foot of water poured over the floor of the bridge. Then Alma and her friends just watched from a safe distance.

Alma tried to tell Mama that she was afraid of the bridge at night. Mama said it was safe now and Alma would have to come.

Sister was just a step ahead of Alma, carrying the lantern. The feeble, shifting light made the black shadows from the heavy timbers move like palpable shapes ready to jump out at them. Alma screamed, "Look out," when shadows like long waving arms reached out to her.

"Shut up. You almost made me drop the lantern." Mama, carrying Brother and walking a step behind, scolded, "Be quiet." Now their footsteps rang out so loud they sounded like the three Billy Goat's Gruff trip-trapping across the bridge. The noise would certainly wake the old Troll, 'with eyes as big as saucers and a nose like a poker'.

The bridge creaked and a chill wind moaned through the old timbers. Alma's whole body shook.

Sorina's house looked dark and deserted, hunched back in the shadows of the bridge. Alma could hear and feel the power of the river as its heavy waters rumbled in the darkness.

Sorina opened the door, holding a candle. The flickering light from the candle made her face look all wavy, like a moving mask. Alma was so frightened she grabbed a handful of her mama's coat. They moved forward in silence to put Brother to bed. The only light in the bedroom was from the candle Sorina now placed before the statue of the Virgin Mary. Alma stayed close to Mama, still holding on to her coat. Sorina broke the silence to scold, "Get away from under your mama's feet. Let her put Baby down. You're not a baby."

Sorina pulled Alma's coat and cap off and shoved her out into the large dining room, where a dim light bulb hung from a long cord, directly over the round table. Tonight Alma would have to sit at the table. Since she was small, Sorina placed Sears Roebuck and Montgomery Ward catalogues under her. They were slippery and hard; her feet dangled and the books cut into her legs.

Sorina ordered Alma to put her hands on the table and stretch her fingers to touch Sister's and Mama's. Sorina turned off the light and said the table would move and there would be knocks and maybe voices from the spirits. No one was to talk except her.

The room was shivery cold and almost black. Alma pressed her hands hard on the table to keep it from moving. Her neck hurt and soon both feet were numb. There was a wavering speck of candle light from the half open bedroom door. Sorina sat hunched over the table, wrapped in her black clothing, mumbling a kind of chant.

Alma thought of Zio. He wouldn't have liked this any more than he liked the fortune telling cards or the dream books. He liked bright cheerful colors and hated to see Sorina dressed in black. He always wore his red plaid jacket and colored shirts.

The first time Brother coughed, Mama started to get up. Sorina muttered, "Don't move. You'll break the spell."

Finally Brother was quiet and Sorina stopped mumbling. Alma squirmed and Mama and Sister pressed their fingers hard against hers to warn her to be quiet and stay awake. She opened her eyes wide and began to look around the large room, so she wouldn't have to watch Sorina and could stay awake. Everyone was still. Alma stared into the stillness.

Suddenly there was Zio, clear across the room. He looked so big, standing there. He didn't move. She watched him with all her might. He began to come slowly toward the table. It took him a long time. When he came closer, she could see he was smiling, as if he were happy again. Slowly, slowly he came until he was across the table from her. Then he held out his arms, as if he were going to pick her up and swing her.

Alma cried out, "Zio, Zio," pulled her hands free from the table and threw herself toward him. The chair slid, the catalogues slipped and she fell.

Alma was shouting, "Zio is here, Zio is here," even before Mama could pick her up. "Look Mama, look." But Sorina turned on the light and Zio wasn't where she pointed. The smile vanished from her face, as Sorina took her from Mama, shoved her shoulders back with hurtful hands and forced her face up.

Sorina demanded, "Did you really see him?"

"Oh, yes. Zio came clear across the room to see me."

"Liar!"

Alma pulled away from Sorina and turned to stand against her mother. "Mama, Zio was here. I really saw Zio."

From the way she smiled and held her, Alma knew that Mama believed her.

Ruby Mae

Nyla

She turned the soap around and around in her hands, allowing the warm water to run. A small bit of warmth. It had been a long time since her hands had been husky pink. The blue had spread and spread. She blinked away the realization that the blue veins in her hands matched the blue around her mouth, pinched now, in the mirror. She sucked in a breath of air, for a moment pushing away the fear.

Straightening up, she pulled her shoulders up and back, trying very hard not to feel the ache down her spine. She patted a few wisps of greying hairs into place, eyes sweeping the mirror for flaws in the rest of her. She whispered to herself, possibly even to the owner of the feet in the toilet stall behind her, "Still spark in them eyes, yet." Her words echoed around the tile floor, bounced off the walls, as she pushed her feet to shuffle out the door, her swollen legs making it difficult to walk the stride she was used to. Before her eyes there was another reflection of her form in the windows dividing the offices from the corridors. Leaning over the drinking fountain, a flash of her own lips, pursing to catch the foul, chemical smelling water. Everything reflected "old woman" back to her. She felt old, but not yet obsolete.

She passed a clock on the way to her desk, the second hand moving as slowly as she felt. Only seven more minutes until coffee break. Then a fifteen minute reprieve from the work, mounting day by day. Continuous.

As she sat in her chair, exhausted from the walk, she peered over her glasses, aware that her supervisor, Gert, had been watching as usual.

Tight lipped, pinched face and hard bitter eyes, Gert kept lists: of people who were tardy; how long and how often they went to the bathroom; of what things she overheard in the bathrooms. Gert used the lists to tattle to the bosses upstairs.

How she disliked Gert! Especially since the time Gert had separated her and her friend, Mattie. They'd gone everywhere together; lunch, coffee breaks and even vacations. Gert hadn't liked their friendship and their talking. Gert's motto was: "You can't talk and get the work done." But Mattie could talk a blue streak while her fingers flew over the paperwork; she could put out more work than even Gert.

She stared straight into Gert's eyes as she sat remembering all those things no one spoke of anymore. The fact was, Gert had gotten the job through the Republican Party. It bothered Gert to hear her and Mattie talk about unions and the Democrats. So it was the content of their talk that upset Gert, rather than the fact that they talked at all. But Gert would never admit it. Therefore, it was predictable that the day after a victorious Republican election, Gert separated her and Mattie.

Mattie was round like a hugable bear—roly, poly and healthy. Everyone had been surprised when Mattie had found out about the cancer growths. Mattie and she had worried about it together. Gert had frowned. Then Mattie went to the hospital. She stopped working for a moment remembering the day when Mattie came back from her leave of absence. Gert told them to be quiet. Again. But Mattie just couldn't take it this time; so she told Gert what she thought after all the years of the hovering, bitching and complaining. Mattie and she had been so proud of each other; Gert had finally been told the truth! Now there were the sad days without her friend Mattie sitting right there beside her; the vacant desk a constant reminder. "Yes," she sighed to herself, "we were the inseparable Mattie and Ruby Mae."

Now it was just her and Gert getting old together. But Gert was boss, and still treated her like a child, telling her what to do, how to do it, always afraid she'd make a mistake. And oh, Gert would make her pay dearly for an error, reminding her weeks later of a mistake in addition somewhere in the piles of work.

Mattie had told her long ago that she must be sick—that something was wrong. But days, months then years went by, and she had done nothing about it. It was Mattie's sickness that finally made her do something about herself. She had worried so much about Mattie. And she'd thought . . . well . . . that Mattie might die. But now Mattie was back to work; happy and taking good care of herself, too. She thought for a moment about how important Mattie had become. There was nobody else who understood her like Mattie did. And Gert had up and separated them. She sat back in her chair making a banging noise as she thought about how much she'd accepted from Gert; all the other mean things she let go by, smoothing things over inside herself. What Gert had done to Mattie was the last and final blow. Gert had known about the cancer, but had gone ahead and been mean. She could only lift her eyes to the clock as her thoughts trailed off and the anger curled around her heart.

The younger women, different these days, were easy enough to work with. She'd feel their sympathy for her age, for her ill health, like a burden. Still she couldn't talk to them like she could Mattie. Though they would hesitate, they'd ask how she was, expecting to hear the details. "They must think that I've always been sickly," she would say to herself. She had learned not to say, like some of the other old women.

She hovered a moment over the papers strewn on her desk, picking up the pen carefully. Head looking down, she wasn't going to let on to anyone that her thoughts might be elsewhere besides this work.

While her hands sped mechanically over the papers, picking, choosing the places to stop and write here and there, she thought about what she had to do. Everyone important in her life was scattered now. Children living in far-away places, phone calls only for Easter, Christmas, sometimes on Sundays; husband dead now a long time it seemed. She began to compose the letter in her head. How to tell them that in three days she'd be in that hospital? How to ask them to stop their busy lives for a short while and come to her to help her tidy up the loose ends of her life? And that's where she usually stopped thinking about it.

She blinked and before she knew it, everything relaxed. Chatter started up. She quickly remembered that if her voice didn't croak so, she'd be chattering too. She chuckled to herself at the fact that today she wouldn't have her head laying down on her desk—perhaps they'd ask questions. Today she was breaking her routine. And on Monday she just wouldn't be here anymore. But it was break time now and time to hurry to finish her letter.

The tension in her body eased up a bit—her hands sought out a different pen. There'd be no other time to write; her boarder at home was curious too. Her heart skipped a beat as she thought about what to say. She started to cough, her choking kind—trying to stifle it. Everyone turned around, and she imagined that their eyes said "Why don't you go home—go away—quit reminding us that if we stay in this place we'll end up just like you." She stopped coughing. Eyes turned away and she felt alone enough to think, to regain her composure. Hands shaking, her ridged veins standing out blue, she pulled out the writing tablet, a little one brought from home. With a fresh piece of paper, a different pen, she started.

Darell,

On Saturday morning I'm going into the hospital. I don't know what they'll find inside of me but after all these years I think I'll let them try to find out what's wrong. Now, you know I don't usually ask you to do much but I have to ask you now, if you will please come to help me with a few things and take me to the hospital. Please don't bring Daisy and the children since I don't think I'll be able to handle all the noise and confusion.

Love
MOM

She looked it over. Short and to the point. She was of the age now where time and space mattered. Life was to be carefully measured and pared down to the essentials—to what really mattered. Exhausted from the stop and go effort, she peeked above her glasses and noticed that she still had five more minutes of the coffee break. Time enough to lay her head down. And removing her glasses, pulling her sweater over her head, she laid like a heap of bones and skin across her desk top.

She laid still there for a minute, perhaps dreaming for she suddenly jerked awake, looking shaken, confused. She reflected on lighting just one more cigarette—her yellowing fingertips touching a moment, knowing it was killing her. But it was all killing her! The jerky bus ride; waiting in the snow and heat every morning and night, sitting in the back, inhaling the foul fumes. And drinking the sour water pumped from the bowels of this monstrous forty-one floor tower. And finally the elevator ride that left her stumbling with aching ear drums everyday. So she lit up the cigarette, waving the match in the air to put it out. She sat there in a cloud of smoke, thoroughly enjoying her one pleasure.

The chatter around her stopped. Break time was over. Time to do work; a momentary rest from her memories of the past and her fears of the next three days. But as a weariness settled over her, she refused it, getting up to go wade through the piles of computer books to find one small number. Just one. And perhaps she'd see Mattie—she'd tell her about the letter and her fears—and Mattie would smile for her, making her glad.

She thought as she walked that she wanted no fan fares, no fake concern from these people. No expensive flower arrangements from their mandatory donations. She'd always hated that. So unfair to celebrate sickness, death.

Maybe it was the only safe way for these people to buy a bit of humanness. But she'd take money—money, people always needed. The thought made a chill sweep over her. The air conditioning—it was cold!

She stumbled her way over the carpets, to the books and back to her desk. No circulation. She was freezing. There'd been a pair of ear muffs (left over from winter) in her desk. She whipped them out of the drawer, covering her ears firmly. She sat there like a statue with ear muffs and sweater on during the heat of the day. The only sign of any life thereafter was the red pen moving slowly across the paper. All noise gone, she was left to herself.

That night she fell asleep during the bus ride home; her head tottering on her shoulders. She had to trudge the four blocks back to her street. It was dark. So fear made her clutch her purse tightly under her arm. As she dragged her feet behind her, an effort at each step, she stopped at a mail box. Dropping the letter carefully inside, she hesitated a moment, unsure of the contents but hoping it would get there in time.

The dim lights inside the grocery store were not beckoning her to buy her dinner this night. She sighed as she passed by, actually looking forward to a rest and to be taken care of; it wasn't unusual to go to bed hungry.

She plodded through the next two days, trying to ignore all the signs that there was indeed something wrong. She and Mattie would talk about it quietly, calmly; Mattie giving her courage to go on, talking about her own cancerous growth; talking about it as if to get rid of it again and again. They'd meet secretly in the bathroom, talking between the stalls when everyone else had left. Or they'd find some hidden corner where no one else could find them . . . they were two old ladies and they hoped no one noticed their absence.

"I was scared to die, Ruby Mae," Mattie would say. "But you know, that fear pushed me and pushed me; it was like a two ton truck comin' up behind me and I got so scared that I had to do somethin' about it. So I decided to go right on livin'. So please Ruby Mae, please, no matter what happens in that ol' hospital there, promise me you ain't goin' to come back here an' work for that ol' Gert. I came back 'cause workin' made me happy. It wasn't killin' me like it is you." And Ruby Mae looked at her carefully thinking about all the things she hadn't done in years. Not working for Gert was an impossible dream; what would she do without the money. It was just a glimmer at the end of a tunnel. There was the hospital to get through first.

She'd forgotten about all the things that made her happy. But Mattie hadn't. What a memory that woman had for remembering all the things she'd told her about her life. So the last day of work Mattie and she sat at Mattie's desk, away from Gert, eating their lunches together, talking some more about the hospital and such. It was almost too painful to listen to.

"What about all those things you were going to do Ruby Mae?" Mattie said. "Remember the plants you started on. And what about that unfinished quilt you told me a-bout—the one for the gran'children? And what about those drawings you started three vacations ago—the ones you told me about because you said you never had time—you didn't have time then, Ruby Mae, but you can finish them now; you don't need so much money. Can't you live on his pension and your retirement from this place? Go ahead, Ruby Mae, promise me you won't come back here?"

She swallowed the lump of fear in her throat and whispered, "O.K. Mattie, I'll promise if you'll come and visit and don't forget all about me. I was plannin' to come back because of the people."

At that, Mattie swelled up and hollered, "The people? Why, Ruby Mae I'm surprised at you. What people are your friends here 'cepting me?"

She thought a moment, and realized that Mattie was right.

At quitting time, she began to pack up her desk. Though in enormous pain by now she felt a sense of relief that it was over and a bit elated to begin a new life, though there was yet an ordeal to go through. As she picked through her few possessions, deciding which to take home and which to throw away, Mattie came and stood beside her; she looked up at her and the way she was standing there, easy like, made her feel that Mattie was a rock that she could lean on for awhile. It made her glad to have her as a friend. As they walked to the elevator, Mattie held her under her arm, the two of them looking like a real team together.

Saturday morning she woke to the rose wallpaper, the birds outside in her tree and the sun shining across the bed. She couldn't move yet. Downstairs she heard the commotion the door made in closing and opening. For a moment she couldn't understand why this disturbance was happening, until Darell walked into her bedroom. She raised her hand a little, flapping it in the air as a greeting, but had nothing to say yet. It was time. It was decided, planned what her life would be for the next month or two. She could feel herself falling into helplessness as Darell bagan to take control of the situation. She laid back momentarily and watched him pull out the suitcase from the closet. Though she hadn't felt like moving, his energy bouyed her up and out of the bed.

They packed her suitcase together while she thought out loud about this and that. Every so often he'd say,

"Mom, you'll be all right," or "Everything will work out O.K. Don't worry." But she wanted to make sure—make him understand how important it all was. She vaguely wished that Mattie were here instead of Darell. It scared her a little to wish for a friend rather than appreciating Darell for his time, away from his family and all. He was her son and everything, but he just didn't understand. Not like Mattie would have.

As they pulled away from the curb, her eyes swept the familiar front porch—the vines just beginning to bud. The only tell-tale sign of her fear was the slight mist that shaded her eyes. They were on their way.

In the hospital she decided very quickly that she'd just let things be. The first two days she did nothing but sleep. By Tuesday morning she received a call from Gert. Somehow the word had leaked out. Gert knew what hospital. Who? She wondered if it had been Mattie. Gert was asking about visiting hours.

The doctors poked and prodded. But she was too afraid to ask. Her lungs seemed filled—she knew that. And it was hard to breathe. Her arms were bluish; they felt prickly as if they were asleep—she knew that too. Each day was a little harder to get through. Losing consciousness periodically, not knowing or caring which doctor or nurse stood around her bed, she lost track of all time. Days must have gone by before she clearly knew who the people were. Every now and then she'd imagine that one of the children was there but upon awakening she'd discover that except for the potted plant and her next door neighbor, she'd been alone.

One day she was awakened by a familiar voice. The voice took her back centuries. And she thought she'd never have to hear it again. As she realized who the voice belonged to, she could feel Gert's presence in the room. Though her lids remained shut, she could feel Gert's eyes peering at her. Gert's eyes sweeping over the tubes hanging from her nose, her hands and coming out from under the blankets. She felt a supreme ache; she did not want Gert in her room.

"Ruby Mae, how are you?" she heard Gert whisper. How could she tell her? But then it didn't really matter to this woman. "The doctors said we almost lost you, but now you're going to pull through." She heard Gert say the words but there wasn't a meaning behind them, so she continued to keep her eyelids shut tightly, incapable of uttering a word, hoping that Gert would leave.

Pretending to be unconscious, she laid clenching her fist under the blankets until tears started to swell underneath her closed lids. Not totally understanding why, she was determined to make that woman leave. But Gert continued to stand there waiting, a contest of wills playing between them, the tension mounting second by second. Finally the woman in the next bed turned to Gert and explained that Ruby Mae just wasn't awake and perhaps she should come back another day. It wasn't until she heard Gert's punctual footsteps fade away down the hall corridor that she peeked around the pillow at her neighbor, giving her a smile and a wink.

The next morning, Mattie was with her when she called the office. In her best voice possible, pretending that she didn't know Gert had already been there, she left the message that she wanted no visitors. And from then on it seemed that every time she regained consciousness, Mattie was sitting beside the bed. Mattie was there to give her courage and make her feel better. Mattie was there to tell her that she looked better, that the swelling was going down, and that her color was coming back. She would go to sleep peacefully after Mattie left for the night.

The last Gert and the other people at the office heard from Ruby Mae, was when she phoned, saying that she wanted no visitors. People talked about that for days. Her desk remained vacant, loaded down with books and papers. No one even bothered to straighten it up; someone must have known that Ruby Mae wasn't coming back.

Word had it that Ruby Mae had a few more bad spells, but pulled through and is now doing just fine. Mattie must remind people of Ruby Mae so they ask her the latest news, perhaps just to make conversation. Everyone's fear of losing their jobs was dampened last week by the hiring of a new person. So gossip flared again that Ruby Mae must have quit for good. A few tried to get the information from Mattie but she remained silent. So people still tried to guess. They wagged their heads and commented, "Do ya' think she quit or retired? What will she do without a job?" Some even tried to figure out how much retirement money she had when she left. They even tried to figure out how much sick leave the State will have to pay her in cash!

A few months passed. No one spoke of Ruby Mae anymore. She was gone. Her office was nearly empty, now that the machines had taken over. Then one day she appeared on the floor, face flushed pink; the only sign she'd been ill was a slight swelling in one leg and the fact that she limped. She moved from desk to desk of the people she'd known and remembered. Some congratulated her. Very few asked her any questions. A few of the older women gathered around offering advice on how to get along on retirement. She refused to discuss it. She looked happy. The only thing she said, and people remembered it for a long time afterward, was, "I almost died in this place. Tell everyone to get out while they can. Getting out will cure anything." And people joked that she was living proof of what this place does to you.

At Ruby Mae's retirement dinner all the old friends were there. And at the office Mattie passed around a huge envelope for contributions. Some came back reporting that Ruby Mae's three sons were there. Others told about what a nice, well mannered family she had, and how Ruby Mae had done so well to raise such wonderful sons; they surely must have been good to her. At that comment, a lady who barely knew Ruby Mae, piped up and offered her opinion, "There were such expensive cars sitting in the parking lot, I thought I was in church! And ya' should have seen the clothes that family had on! I bet they're all professionals. Didn't someone say her boys went to College? Well I bet that's how Ruby Mae is able to retire!"

Mattie, who had been standing aside during the conversation proudly explained, "They sure enough weren't around when Ruby Mae was dyin' in that hospital—or when she was a workin' here—I was!" Everyone turned to go back to their desks, conversation stopping abruptly at that comment; after all Mattie must have known what she was talking about. And for once—there was nothing more to say about Ruby Mae. By now she is totally forgotten!

The Light

Linnea A. Due

Tracy Malone was known around Sarah Lawrence as the biggest drunk in a school full of boozers. She'd vault over barbed wire fences, ripped out of her mind, fall on her face in classes, barely manage to crawl down to the cafeteria for a cup of coffee on a hungover, grey morning. But Trace never struck me as sad, because her death-beckoning comforted me somehow, like there was some peace to be found in a nervous world. All her energy was trapped deep inside her, so she glowed from within, a quiet child's light, not that quick, frenetic sunburst Sarah Lawrence girls are famous for. Tracy never expected or gave approval, so when I was around her, I could be myself.

When I talked to other people, I felt like I was trying to grab hold of one of those bouncy, plastic balls that change shape when they hit something. I'd try to make them solid, and in the trying, I'd go fuzzy and shapeless myself. No one seemed to have a form in all that springy plastic but Tracy. She'd given up so long ago she never felt frightened. She never had to retreat into an amorphous mass like the rest of us.

I liked to watch her out my window, swinging across the lawn in her peajacket, hooting on her kazoo, small and cocky, ready to punch out the first fucker that laid a hand on her. Sitting there at my window, I grinned at her swagger, and then a quiet would steal into me, and for awhile I could forget about me and all the other frenzied people.

45

Strange we were all so scared. But we looked at Sarah Lawrence as if the college was the calm before the storm of marriages, careers, times when we really would be all alone. The worst was not knowing what to expect. We didn't know who was going to be happy, who was going to fail, who was going to go crazy. I kept thinking if I could just see a picture of myself at thirty, a little three-minute short, even if I was hooking in some scummy east side bar, at least then I'd know. We were all tired of waiting, and we jostled each other like nervous racehorses at the gate, only the gate lasted four long years rather than a couple of minutes. Tracy was the only calm one in the field. Her life's ambition was to be dead from drink at twenty-five, and when I saw the light that shone out of her face at twenty, I figured she'd made a good choice.

I first met Tracy one night at the bar in Bronxville. She was drinking shots of house whiskey, singing to the juke box, when she grabbed at her stomach like she wanted to yank it out. Another girl and I dragged her to the bathroom, thinking she wanted to throw up, but she was crying and still clawing at her stomach, so we loaded her in my car and hauled her up the hill to school. I ran down to the cafeteria and got a bottle full of milk, while her friend pumped Mylanta into her until she stopped sobbing. I stayed on after the friend left, sitting next to the bed, holding her hand, unwilling to let go of her. When she opened her eyes, I said: "We brought you home." She nodded and clasped my hand tighter. "I'm Tracy Malone," she whispered. "Marty," I said quietly.

She nodded again. "I know." Her eyes closed, and I sat there watching her sleep. After awhile, I let myself out into the early dawn and walked back to my room, strangely content, listening to my feet crunch through the dried-out snow.

This year, my senior year, she lived in my dorm, in the room directly above me. Sometimes she'd stomp on her floor, and we'd split a fifth of whiskey up in her room. We were drinking buddies now, me and Tracy and Beka and Maggie, a small band of rebels who only left the campus to go down to the bar in town. We never talked to each other much, any of us, but only Tracy's face shone with that unearthly glow. The rest of us knew that pretty soon our ambitions were going to get the better of us, and we'd be off and running. Every day that year, at 10:15, I stood at my window, even when Beka and I were lovers, so I could watch Tracy walk down to the art building. It always made me smile, the way she swaggered like a cowboy, her feet set wide apart, looking like she was hustling down to the old corral to wipe out Dirty Dan.

When Beka moved out of my room in the winter of the year, she and Tracy began a week-long drunken binge that ended with all of Beka's clothes in Tracy's room. Tracy left for the weekend, saying nothing to anyone, and when she got back, Beka still sat in her room, strumming on her guitar.

The next day, the hall phone rang, and I stumbled out of my room to answer it. I heard Beka's husky monotone, like a cracked record at slowed-down speed.

"What the fuck you calling me on the campus line for?" I said. "I was asleep. Anyhow, you're just one flight up." When she didn't answer, I snarled: "Well, aren't you?"

"Yeah," she mumbled, and I could almost see her shifting around on the carpet, a big, nervous lion. "I didn't want to see you, see. I mean, I wanted to tell you something, and I wanted to tell you on the phone, since, uh, we were, uh, sleeping together and all."

"What does that have to do with the phone?" I asked

but my hand made a funny jump that pulled the cord to
its limit.

"I just wanted to tell you, I mean, since we never talked
about what was going to happen . . . between us, I mean,
well, Tracy and me are sleeping together, and I'm going to
be living up here now." She finished in a rush of words, and
I concentrated on reading the graffiti on the cardboard
backing of the telephone booth.

"We never talked at all," I said finally, and we hung on
there for a second, two drowning swimmers senselessly
clutching each others' lifelines, and then the phones clicked
at the same time. I walked back to my room, hearing the
echo of Beka's footsteps directly above me, hearing her
open Tracy's door while I opened mine. I picked up my
chemistry notebook and flipped through it, listening as
hard as I could for sounds over my head. I sat there maybe
two minutes in all, and then I laid my notebook on the
dresser and stalked down to the cafeteria, glad for once of
the noise and the hurrying people.

I didn't feel like staying in my room much for days afterwards, so I wandered around the campus, pissed and lost,
drinking a lot of coffee, speed-talking to friends, playing
bridge in the all-night tournaments in the administration
building. Sometimes I'd see Tracy walking around, huddled
in Beka's army jacket, her face dark and strained. I had to
lean on my window sill now when she passed by to her
10:15 class. Her darkness made me tired. Beka looked the
same, the big lion, boxed in by her silence and her pride.

Finally I got sick of speeding, so I went into town to
drink myself down. It was the quarter break for some colleges, and the bar was crowded. I went into the deserted
back room. Beka sat there in a booth, her long legs propped

up on the seat in front of her, and she waved me over.

"Lemme get a beer," I said, and I hurried back out front to the mob scene. I hesitated at the bar, trying to decide whether I should go to the piano lounge across the street, but it housed all the thirty-year-old Bronxville wife-swappers, and I didn't feel like being flirty-cute, even vaguely. So I got my beer, pushed through the crowd, and swung into the booth next to Beka, thinking: If you go to a small school, it's wiser to be friends with your former lovers.

"How ya doin'?" I asked, determined to be on the offensive for once.

"Fucked." She swallowed a shot of house whiskey and followed it by half a draft. A waitress peeked out of the kitchen, and Beka waved at her empty glass. Women always leapt out of the woodwork whenever Beka was around, a conjuring trick I never attempted to duplicate.

I chugged down some Bud. "Why fucked?"

Beka avoided my sideward glance and mumbled into the table: "I'm worried about Tracy," like she was embarassed to be worried about someone. I gave her time to recover herself. "Well, what's she doing?"

"Drinking." She shoved around her change in sharp angles.

"Jesus, Beka, Tracy always drinks. Always has."

"Well, this—" She shut up when the waitress came and flashed her big, white grin, the lion at her best. The white-smocked woman, young and Italian, smiled while Beka rubbed her palm sensuously on her tee-shirted belly. I watched as she smiled wider and bit her lip, mesmerized by Beka's slowly circling hand. I sighed and turned to scan the menu on the far wall, but at my motion, the waitress cleared her throat. "You girls watch your language tonight, now." Her voice was too jaunty.

"Well, shee-it," Beka drawled, and the woman giggled and hurried back into the kitchen.

"Probably a mafioso's daughter," I said darkly. "Probably wake up with ten machine gun bullets in your gut."

"In that case, I wouldn't wake up." She sipped at her shot.

"All right," I said. "We were talking about Tracy."

She nodded, serious and back to business. "Her drinking. It's outrageous. She's drinking Irish."

That might mean one of two things, so I said: "Whiskey, or following her forbears?"

"Both. Also, she's not eating." She waved my mouth closed. "I know she never eats. But this time she really isn't. She's lost twenty pounds since I moved into her room."

"God. A skeleton. She never was fat." I pinched the bridge of my nose, to hide my smile and to look thoughtful. I wondered how Beka was going to react to what I planned to say. "Listen, Beka, maybe she's freaked out because it's a gay thing. I mean, your being a woman and all."

Beka was shocked. "Oh, no, that would be really fucked, no, I'm sure she's not freaked about that, that would be stupid."

Our backs were to the door, so when Tracy said, "What would be stupid?", we both jumped.

Beka took a deep breath and watched Tracy move around in front of us, cradling a draft at her side. "Well, we were just saying it'd be stupid . . . I mean . . . Well, listen, Tracy, if you're losing all this weight and stuff because of me, well—"

Tracy laughed a death rattle that said: "Don't flatter yourself." Then she tossed her beer into Beka's face and walked out the door.

The smirking waitress brought a towel, and I ordered two more beers. When Beka was half-way dry, I couldn't resist grinning at her. "Well," I said. "It may not be because of a gay thing."

She rolled her eyes towards the ceiling. "That doesn't mean it's still not because of me."

"Touche," I said, and since she'd thought of that all by herself, I decided to buy the next round.

A few nights later was the dinner before the big play of the year. The school had sprung for wine, and somebody had bought a keg of beer. There was even a vase of flowers on every table. Tracy was supposed to sit with the cast, since she was in the play, but when I stepped out of the snow into the noise, she was huddled next to Beka, dark and tense. Beka and Maggie were toasting the school's benevolence with glasses of wine. I filled up my dish and set it down at their table. "Steak," I said. "I thought this place was bankrupt."

"Yeah, but it's shitty steak," Maggie said. "And no seconds." Her hair was falling over her face, and her eyes were big and bright, like a drunken owl trying to maintain some semblance of propriety.

"Better than liver," I said. We ate, Beka and Maggie taking turns crossing to the keg when the wine ran out. On Beka's third trip, she set down four glasses of beer, and Maggie drained hers at a single gulp. She tried to hand her glass back to Beka.

Beka laughed. "Fuck that shit," she said. "It's your turn."

Maggie grabbed the vase of flowers, dumped out the water and the stems, and stumbled off, holding the vase loosely at her side. She strode back a few minutes later, dribbling a trail of beer from the top of the vase. "Here," she said. "This oughta help." She slumped down in her chair and glared at Tracy's stoney face. "What's your problem, Tracy? You're hardly even drinking."

"She's in the play," Beka explained.

"Hell, I know she's in the play," Maggie said. "What's that got to do with drinking? I'm in the audience, and I'm drinking."

I laughed, but no one else did. Maggie hitched herself forward, her elbows planted on either side of her plate. "I been wanting to talk to you anyway, Tracy. You look like shit. Everytime I see you, you look like somebody just walked up and stuck a knife in your gut."

"Maybe that's cause she saw you, Maggie," Beka said. Beka and Maggie glared at each other, drawing some invisible lines, and I watched Tracy push her half-eaten steak around with her fork.

"It's true," Maggie insisted, staring at Beka. "It's fucking true. And ya know when it was Tracy started looking so shitty was when you—"

"Shut up," Beka said.

"Oh, fuck off, Beka. I'm talking to Tracy, not to you."

"It didn't look that way to me." Both of them sipped at their beers, and I noticed several tables around ours had quieted down to listen. Tracy was huddling further into her jacket, her eyes stubbornly glued to her plate.

Maggie turned back to her. "It's true, Tracy. You started being all weird when Beka moved in. Beka's bad—"

I blinked just once, but in that second, Beka had gotten around the table and dragged Maggie half-way to the door. When I got outside, Beka was sitting astride Maggie in the snow, slapping her face back and forth. They were both absolutely silent, and the sound of the slaps ricochetted across the white paths. "Stop it," I said, grabbing at Beka's arm. She got up willingly, her eyes confused, and she ran off up the hill.

I leaned over Maggie and wiped away a thin trickle of blood from her lip.

"It's true." Maggie mumbled. "It's true. Beka's bad for her." I helped her up, and she kept repeating, "Beka's bad for her," until I got tired of it.

"Look," I said. "It's none of our business. Besides, what are you so upset about? You've been acting all jealous since they got together."

She pulled away from me and sagged against a railing. "Fuck you, Marty. Fuck you! You got nothing to say. You've been sniffing around Tracy for two years, so just shut up! Fuck all of you!" She threw her arms out wide, her face contorted, and then she stumbled off towards her dorm. I walked back inside the cafeteria, but Tracy had faded away, leaving her steak on the table.

The next day, Tracy cut off her hair. She did it in a very Sarah Lawrency way. She stuck her head alongside a paper-cutter in the yearbook room, reached her arm around, and pulled the blade down to the nape of her neck. She left her hair laying on the white crosshatches, and the janitor bitched about it all week.

Her hair didn't look too bad, considering it all hung in a clump. She still huddled around, dark and gloomy, hugging herself in Beka's jacket, but now she wore blue sunglasses she'd taken from my room when I wasn't there. I saw her wearing them in the cafeteria.

"Hey," I said, balancing my tray on my knee. "Aren't those mine?"

She looked at me blankly for a moment and then pointed to the glasses. "These? Oh, yeah, they are." I stood next to her for a minute, holding my tray, feeling stupid. When she didn't say anymore, I finally walked away.

That weekend, Beka went to Washington to see an old

friend. I drove to the liquor store, bought a bottle of Jack Daniels, and knocked on Tracy's door. She flung it open and stood framed in the doorway, her legs wide apart.

I held up the bottle and realized how skinny she really was, now that she wasn't wrapped up in that big jacket. I could see her shoulder blades sticking out through her tee-shirt.

She motioned me inside and shut the door. "Beka's in Washington," she said. I nodded and looked around at all the black Nietzche quotes covering the walls while she kept her eyes on the bottle. "You come to bitch about your sunglasses?"

I opened the fifth and handed it to her. "No. I came to bitch about the fact you haven't said a word to me in two months."

She shrugged and drank out of the bottle. "You know me," she said, not apologetically, just like her actions were out of her control.

I shrugged too and poured some whiskey in a glass sitting by her bed. She moved around restlessly, tossing some of Beka's books in a corner, putting on a record. I sat down on her old mattress laying on the floor. The frame stood abandoned in the hall outside.

"Maggie was here all afternoon," Tracy said. "She was ranting about this and that, and then she started this long rap about how bad Beka is for me." She fixed me with two cold blue eyes. "That what you're here for, too? Some kind of planned-out campaign? The League to Save Tracy from Beka?"

I ignored all that. "No," I said. "I just wanted to see you."

"Oh." She sat down and we watched each other drink. She lit a cigarette and sighed. "The thing is, Marty, I just want to live my life. I don't want anybody fucking with it. Taking care of me."

"Who wants to take care of you?" I scoffed.

"Well, you and Maggie. And Beka, but a lot less. It's your big trip. You get off on it, you only feel good when you're protecting somebody. Like when my stomach was fucking up last year. I bet you felt good."

"Oh, fuck," I said. "So that's why you're going with Beka? She's so damned unprotective?"

"Fuck you, Marty. 'Going with Beka'. It sounds like junior high school. Anyhow, what makes you think you could do any better?" She spat it out at me, and I moved back involuntarily. "I mean, Beka comes into my life, she goes out, that's it. I like her. Maybe I even love her. But I don't want anyone messing around with my life!"

"Poor Tracy," I said bitterly. "Sure is a drag having a lover. Now you've got responsibilities."

I didn't think she was even listening, staring out her window, but she spun around and yelled: "Responsibilities! Yeah! You're the big responsible one. You're thinking: 'I'll take care of you, Tracy. Everything'll be fine if you'll only go with me!' You think I opened myself up by letting Beka move in here. Well, I didn't. It was her decision. And when she splits, it'll be her decision! Don't look at me like that!"

I had pasted a grin on my face, and I was nodding at her like she was some sort of crazy child having a temper tantrum. It was the only thing I could think of to do. Part of my head wanted to say: well, so take a chance with me, Tracy, and another part was scared to death of her. I couldn't imagine that I'd ever felt good, here in her room. I got up slowly and left, my back stiff, carrying her glass with me.

When I got outside the dorm, I pitched the glass against a brick wall and listened to it shatter. I wanted to yell, but I couldn't decide who I was yelling at, and it seemed stupid to scream out loud to myself. So I climbed the barbed wire fence encircling the campus and rapped at the window of Maggie's room in one of the converted houses across the street. Someone groaned, and I rapped again, harder.

Maggie raised the window and peered out, blinking. "Whadya want?"

"You wanta sleep with me?"

"No, you crazy? I'm asleep."

"O.K." I sauntered off, climbed the fence, and went back to my room, I could hear Tracy playing Big Pink through the window. My suitemate came in from a date, and I started dealing out cards for gin rummy when Maggie walked in without knocking. She hadn't brushed her hair, and it hung in tangles down the back of her workshirt. "Come on," she said. "I changed my mind." I followed her out, waving at Jody, my suitemate. Maggie added over her shoulder as I closed the door: "I've gotta bottle of gin."

Two days later, I decided Tracy was fucking me over, so I went up to her room to demand my sunglasses. A token gesture, but I figured I'd feel better. I just walked in, to avoid a repeat of Tracy posed in her doorway. I squinted through the smokey gloom and saw Tracy shaking on her bed, wrapped in a blanket, two empty fifths on the floor, and a half-full pint perched on the window ledge. Her face was white and sweaty. I walked past her into the bathroom and wet a towel, wringing it out, trying not to shake myself. I knelt in front of her and wiped off her face.

"Don't talk," I said when she mumbled something. So she raised her fist and held it in front of her, mute. I unwrapped the bloody washcloth and bit the inside of my mouth. I swallowed fast to get rid of the taste.

"This needs stitches, Tracy."

"Butterfly stitches in bathroom."

I walked into the bathroom again and rummaged around until I found the box of little white butterflies. I poured some warm water into a bowl and got another clean towel. Both of us were shaking so bad it was hard washing her hand without hurting her. "Glass," she mumbled.

"What?" I was bent over, trying to hold the flesh together while I put on the first bandage.

"Did you get all the glass out?" She sounded better.

I started all over again, flushing the cuts out with more warm water and dragging her desk lamp over so I could see better. "No glass," I announced, and she held one side of her hand, and I pressed with the other, and together we managed to set four bandages across the deepest cuts. I figured her knuckles would heal by themselves.

"Fuck," she said. "I didn't think it would do that. Do you think the school'll get really pissed?"

"Where was it?"

. We were both talking in whispers, like the administration had spies listening under every door.

"One of those main windows in the front of the cafeteria. The big ones. I was coming up from the bar, and I was just pissed. Do you think they'll know?"

"Nah. Even if somebody saw you, they wouldn't tell. Unless it was a guard, and he would've come up right away. One time last year, right after the Christmas party, I chiseled the lock off the cafeteria door 'cause I knew they stored the left-over sherry there. Nobody ever said anything."

Tracy nodded slowly. "Did you get the sherry?"

"Sure. Isn't Beka back yet?"

"No."

I shuttled over to the record player in the silence and put

on Big Pink. I lay half-off and half-on the bed, and Tracy took my hand in her good one. I couldn't imagine ever being scared of her. We rested there, peaceful and comfortable, until Beka threw the door open with a crash that woke up half the dorm.

While all these people were screaming: "Shut up, Goddamnit," I watched, blank, as Beka's face went surprised, shocked, furious, and then as blank as mine. She shook her head. She was so drunk she could hardly stand up.

"What'd you do to your hand, Trace?" Each word sounded like she'd wrenched it out from underneath a rock.

I felt I was fading off somewhere, but when Tracy said: "Put it through a window," I jolted back. Beka stormed outside, slamming the door again. We lay back, and I said: "I think I'd better go," but I didn't move.

Beka opened the door quietly this time and crossed to the bottle on the ledge. She gulped some whiskey, sloshing it around in her mouth, and then she stepped into the bathroom. I could hear glugging noises in the sink. She shoved open the bedroom window and flung the bottle into the street below. Then she turned to us and said: "No more drinking," while I said, "I'm going." In the background, twenty women screamed: "Shut the fuck up!"

Everything quieted, and Tracy muttered "Stay" and squeezed my hand. Someone knocked on the door, and Beka opened it to my suitemate Jody, who apologized and explained that Maggie had woken her up, asking for me, and would I please come down and do something about her?

Beka said, "Christ, she too ripped to walk up the stairs herself?

Jody stared at Beka like she was a walking freak show, and I saw what Jody saw: Beka drunk, Beka punched-out, her eyes wild, Tracy hunched over behind her, cradling her gashed hand in her lap.

I jumped up before Beka could answer that stare. "Pardon me," I said, and followed Jody out of the room. The lock clicked before we were two steps away.

I got down to some studying then, and just an occasional game of bridge with the people on my floor. It had somehow turned into the middle of April, and senior activities were starting soon. But I kept hearing rumors about Tracy. Maggie collared me one day in the cafeteria and told me Tracy was transferring to some college in the midwest no one had ever heard of. "What's that supposed to prove?" I said irritably. I felt vaguely upset, as though people were doing things they weren't supposed to do. Even though I was graduating in another month, I wanted everything else to stay the same.

"Nothing," Maggie said. "Why should it prove anything?"

I shrugged. "I don't know. It's just weird. I mean, why would she leave?"

"Why wouldn't she leave?" Maggie countered.

"Fate, I guess. It's fated that all this shit happen here. You can't run out on it."

Maggie laughed. "You always think fate stops at a certain point. You want to draw the curtain down and say 'O. K., everybody! That's it! We're all stuck with each other, so make the best of it.' It doesn't work that way. People come and people go."

I ignored that. I'd heard it so often it meant as much to me as wine being Christ's blood. I changed the subject.

Then late one night as I was walking to the library to slip a book through the return slot, I saw a little brown bundle underneath one of the elms. When I got closer, I realized it was Tracy, leaning against the tree trunk, wrapped up in an army blanket.

"Whatcha doin', Trace?" I flung myself down beside her and immediately jumped back up. "Shit, it's wet down there. Aren't you wet?"

She shook her head, looking dreamy and peaceful. The glow was flooding back into her face. She stuffed her hand under the blanket and pulled out a hip flask. She poked it at me, and I shook my head. "No, but look, Tracy, you should probably come inside." She drank out of the flask silently, and I finally went back to my room.

I stared out the window until I noticed drops blurring my vision. I shrugged into my jacket and went back outside. Tracy was asleep, wrapped like a cocoon in her blanket, and the rain looked fresh and clean on her face. I hunkered down beside her and watched her sleep, like I'd done the night I met her. Once I almost touched her cheek, but I was afraid I'd make the darkness clamp down on her again. So I started walking around, just looking at the campus, and I realized during that walk that if I just dropped some speed and wrote my papers, I could be out of college in three days. I'd skip all the graduation stuff, all the parties and the tears and drunken brawls, and drive back to California by some long, quiet route. I felt peaceful then, thinking about driving, just me to listen to. I crossed the campus to my dorm, looking up through the dawn to the elm. Tracy was gone.

But by the end of the three days, I was starting to see things, and I still hadn't packed yet. So I crashed for four-teen hours and packed the next day. No one was around, because it was a Saturday, and there was a demonstration in New York. I thought of leaving notes on Maggie's and Tracy's doors, but I couldn't think of anything to say, so I just got in my car and drove through the front gates, feeling like I was in some dream. But half-way down the hill, I saw Beka trudging up from the train station. I pulled over to the side of the road, and she came up to the car window. "I'm leaving," I said.

"You're not staying for graduation?"

"No."

"And you're leaving now. You're all packed and everything."

I nodded. We lit cigarettes and looked out at the road. "Well," she said finally, "I guess I better get on up to school."

"Yeah," I said, glad she'd broken the silence, "I better get going too." We both looked away, because we knew there was no reason either of us had to go anywhere. I suddenly couldn't think of one thing I wanted to do for the rest of my life, maybe fifty years, and I was terrified, facing all that emptiness. Beka looked up in time to see the fear cross my face, and she patted me clumsily on the arm.

"Tell Tracy and Maggie I said goodbye," I said quickly, as afraid of her caring as I was of the emptiness.

"Oh, sure," she said. "I'll tell 'em."

I put the car in gear and she started walking, and all of a sudden I was driving away. The moment I got on the thruway, all my plans for a quiet drive back snapped into frantic lane changing and speed. I drove straight through, as if a big, hungry dog were nipping at my heels, and if I stopped, he'd get me.

Charm School

Sandy Boucher

"I'd be careful about going too far up that way," the woman says to Ellen. "There's a man up that way — a real sicky."

Ellen glances up the beach to where the figure of a man is visible in the thin fog, and two dogs leaping near him in the surf.

But the woman shakes her head. "No, he's wandering around up on the cliffs. I mean, some of these guys I don't mind, but *this* one scared me!" She gestures as she talks, and the wrinkles in her forehead knot. "I was sitting there doing my meditation when he climbed down off the cliff. He came over and asked me if I wanted some company. I said, 'No, I do not!' He just stood there, and then he said, 'Show me your nipples'."

Ellen and the woman exchange a look of shock, and then the woman mimes her anger, lifting a clenched fist and pushing away from her body with it. "Well, I turned to him and I said, 'You go away! Get away from here!' "

Ellen looks up to search the cliffs for a glimpse of him.

They rise steeply from the beach, their packed sand ochre and tan and sienna, and on top the grass spikes up like hair.

"A real sicky. You know, if I were a young girl I'd expect to be approached, but I'm an older lady!"

When the woman has gone, Ellen stands looking in the opposite direction, back toward the Cliff House, but the tide is so high there that the beach is covered with water. No chance of going that way.

"Damn!" she says.

Lowering her head, she begins walking slowly along under the cliffs. "He's not gonna drive me away!" she decides, and shoves her fists deep into the pockets of her jacket. But already the knowledge of his presence has slid like a screen between her and her surroundings. Thoughts rise in her like garbage from the bottom of a pond — sights she would rather forget, stories told by women in the coffee room at work, by her other friends. And she thinks of children. At what young age will a girl child hear that husky, whispered "Hey . . . look!" and turn to see the man in the darkened doorway, the man back among the trees, the man in the window. It is her own adolescent self she would like to shield against what happened long ago. But the memory is a hot probe in her.

Ellen kicks at a piece of seaweed shaped like the brown rubber bulb of a syringe. Scuffing her feet in the sand, she glances at the cliffs which rear up, gouged and grooved by weather. Is that a movement up there, or is it just the wind ruffling the grass? She watches for a time, seeing no one.

It is years since she has thought of Zangaro. She plods down the beach, her hands clasped behind her, knowing it is the man up on the cliffs who has plunged her into these thoughts, and hating him for it.

The summer Ellen was seventeen, a Charm School and

Modeling School opened in Minneapolis where she lived with her family. No such establishment had ever existed in that solid and businesslike town, and a lot of press coverage was given to its offices in a downtown hotel and to its owner, a Mr. Henri Zangaro from New York City.

From these newspaper articles Ellen's parents got the idea that Mr. Zangaro's charm school would be the answer to what they defined as her "problem." She had not been popular in the high school from which she had just graduated; in fact, she had been miserable and ignored for those four years. Ellen knew it had been because she came from the wrong part of town each day to attend that school in a prosperous suburb, because her father was not a doctor or a businessman but a machinist in a factory, because she wore cheap nylon sweaters while the others wore cashmere or suede.

But she had no words to tell her parents this. Surely they must have known it themselves. Yet now they wanted to help her, having watched her suffer through those four years — and especially they were anxious that she should succeed in finding a husband.

So Ellen's mother, with unusual initiative, inquired by phone of the Charm School to see if they needed a typist, and arranged that Ellen could work out her tuition at the school by doing typing at night after her regular job in an office downtown. Secretly she was hurt that her parents saw her as deficient and in need of fixing up, yet she was grateful to them too for trying to help her. She would not, herself, have chosen such a school, but since it had been arranged, she agreed to go.

Mr. Zangaro had what amounted to a harem. He was surrounded by young women whom he handled and groomed, cutting their hair, giving them lessons in makeup, telling them how to stand, to sit, how to act toward men ("When a man is lighting your cigarette, look up into his eyes over the flame."), what kind of girdle to buy, what clothes to wear. Obediently, Ellen did all she was told to do, feeling strangely dislocated.

And since she was there with Mr. Zangaro in the office several hours every evening typing the promotional letters, he talked to her about himself. He had grown up in Hell's Kitchen in New York, had started out by making sketches on the street and various other hustles. By sheer ruthlessness and a crude charm that came mostly from his sexual curiosity and erotic awareness of women, he had worked his way up in the beauty business. And of course he changed his first name of Gaetano to the requisite French name, and became Henri.

A short, square man, with stubby hands, he was tough, and proud of how far he had raised himself from his poor beginnings. His little eyes were sharp and knowing. He had a wide mouth, with lips that were sensual and cruel, over widespaced, tobacco-stained teeth. It was a mouth that fell most naturally into a sneer.

Sometimes as Ellen was typing he would stand peering at her and then say, "Ellen, you need a trim. Come in the back." And obediently she went behind the partition with him and sat down in the barber's chair. Then he would clip and pat her hair. She saw him in the mirror, his little eyes, squinted against the smoke from the Old Gold that almost always hung on his lip, gazing proprietarily at her head. He talked about the models he had known in New York — one in particular who had been a stunning creature, chased by numbers of men, who would have none of them because she was a lesbian. He shook his head. The idea fascinated him. This is life, he was saying to Ellen, I'm telling you what life is about. And then he would go into one of his lectures. "Something like a pimple on a girl's nose — just one little pimple — can turn a man off completely." He talked about his wife, the latest one, whom he had acquired when he came to Minneapolis. "She has a master's degree in literature," he told Ellen. And it was obvious what a triumph it had been for him to marry this woman who had "culture." She was now at home bearing his children — two so far.

In these hours when they were alone in the office, there was something established between them. It was something Ellen did not seek and did not want, but *he* was in charge there, and she had been so successfully trained into respect for authority, beginning with her father, that her only manner of resistance was to withdraw. In this situation in which he controlled the space and the interchange between them, withdrawing did no good. During classes or when others were in the office, he was brisk and businesslike to her, but when they were alone, he drew her into his circle of energy, played on her innocence, talked mostly of sex: he was certain it was the moving force for everyone. He was inexhaustibly fascinated by it.

Rough and cynical, he let it be known that he was honoring Ellen by treating her as a friend. And he was going to help her move up in the world. One day his prize pupil came in to visit. She was just back from New York City where she worked as a photographer's model. She was almost six feet tall and weighed 115 pounds. A photograph, Zangaro had told Ellen, puts on twenty pounds. So obviously a photographer's model must be at least twenty pounds underweight. Ellen found this young woman distressing to look at. Poised, superbly elegant, she was so emaciated that the veins stood out on her wrists and ankles like blue worms over the bones. She was strangely languid, speaking in a slow flat voice. She told Zangaro she was in town to get her teeth capped and see her family, and she brought out some folded papers from her big model's bag and showed him the magazine spreads in which she had been featured.

When she had gone, Zangaro said, "She makes a lot of money. You could do it too. You've got the bones."

Ellen didn't want to do it. What she really wanted was to go to college, even though her parents had not let her take the college preparatory course in high school but had insisted she take the commercial course. That meant that while the others studied Latin and French she studied typewriting and basic bookkeeping. She did not blame her parents, they were merely being practical; the training had made it easy for her to get a job as a typist.

A visitor who came often to the office, though he seemed to have no particular business to transact, was an enormous meaty man with slicked-down platinum-bleached hair — a professional wrestler. Zangaro became almost obsequious in his presence, laughing with hysterical urgency at the jokes the man made, saying over and over to anyone who was present, "Isn't he a gas?" This behavior puzzled Ellen, for Zangaro maintained a consistently tough and sneering manner with everyone else.

"I went out with this girl," began the man, with a smirk on his beefy face to indicate this was to be a funny story. "She was a hunchback. I didn't like that, so I took her to a graveyard and I dug a grave and put the hunch in it. And that was the end of that."

"Dug a grave!" sputtered Zangaro. "Put the hunch in it!" And he rocked with harsh laughter. "You hear that, Ellen?" He gripped the big man's arm, doubled over with hilarity.

Ellen stared at them, repelled. She tried to smile, but couldn't. She saw nothing funny in what the man had said, and it only made her more aware that this place was alien territory. In another few weeks her charm course, and thus the job, would be finished, and she would never have to sit here again.

Then one evening the daytime secretary was there doing a special project, using the desk, and Zangaro said, "Okay, let's go upstairs to work, Ellen. I wanta go over this next batch of letters with you." He opened the door, told the secretary to hold all calls for the next hour, and went briskly out into the hall.

Ellen followed, wondering where they were going, glanced back through the glass door at the secretary sitting at the front desk. She followed Zangaro into the elevator, where he stood gazing sternly before him, in a hurry, businesslike. At the seventh floor the elevator stopped. They got out, and Ellen followed Zangaro down the hotel corridor past numbered doors. At one of them he stopped, inserted a key, opened it and motioned her in.

Ellen had never been in a hotel room. When her family traveled to see relatives, they covered the distance in one day; they were not the kind of people who stayed in hotels.

"Phew! Hot!" Zangaro said, and went to open the window.

The room was dull, perfunctory, furnished with a double bed, two chairs, a small glasstopped desk. Traffic noise came in through the window Zangaro had opened.

Ellen stood holding the papers they had come to look at, feeling extremely uncomfortable. That intimacy that had been established between her and Zangaro seemed suddenly stifling. But he was arranging the two chairs before the desk, his motions quick and matter-of-fact.

It was a summer evening, one of those in which the heat does not lift when the sun goes down. Ellen had been at work all day in an office. Her clothes felt sticky and too small; her feet had swollen a little, puffing up so that the edges of her pumps cut into her flesh. Her girdle and hose bound her damply, the stockings pulling behind the knees.

She sat down in the chair next to Zangaro, seeing his rough brown hair, his rough lined skin filmed with sweat. There were brown hairs curling on the backs of his stubby hands.

He explained to her what he wanted in the letters, how he wanted them to look. They worked for about fifteen minutes, and then he sank back in his chair and pulled out a handkerchief to wipe his forehead. His suit coat was open, his tie pulled down from his unbuttoned collar.

"Jesus, my legs hurt," he said, gripping his short thick fingers on his knees, rubbing them. "I been standing all day today." And then he turned his chair to face her. "Here, see what you can do."

She looked at him, not understanding.

"C'mon, give 'em a rub. Help me out." He reached to lift her hands and place them on his knees. "That's right, rub. Come on."

His manner said, This is all perfectly ordinary. There is nothing unusual about it.

Ellen sat with her hands on his knees, looking at his face. He was staring past her, his lips curved into a disdainful smile. The sound of automobiles came through the opened window, the twilight was a transparent grey blue. She felt the moisture on her sides under her clothes.

Slowly, she began to rub his knees. "Harder," he said, "dig in a little." She tightened her fingers, kneading.

"Aaah, that's good," he said, and he closed his eyes and leaned back in the chair. "Right. That's right."

Ellen looked up past his spread thighs to his short torso

relaxed in the chair, his forearms propped on the chair arms.

The room filled up with a silence then, under the traffic hum. He looked as if he were sleeping.

She rubbed his knees.

"Higher," he said, "up a little higher. Ah, yes, that's good."

Her hands moved now on the big muscles of his thighs. It was as if she were hypnotized, part of her standing aside to watch herself do this. She tried to think of a way to stop, but each time she slowed her hands, he said, "No, don't stop. Aaah, feels good." He did not open his eyes to look at her, he did not move, his hands did not touch her. Instinctively she knew that if she stopped or objected he would laugh at her, he would make her feel like a fool for imagining this to be something that it wasn't.

She kneaded the thighs, watched the hands reach to unbuckle the belt, pull the zipper down a little while he sighed.

"Higher," he said, and she moved her hands up a little more, closer to his groin. Now she could see the thick ridge there.

He began to breathe strangely, a kind of snorting in his nose, that he was trying to control, and the swelling under the zipper of his pants got bigger.

Ellen was locked here, caught between what she was seeing and his nonchalant manner that forbade her to define it. She sweated, and her back hurt from leaning over his legs, but she was afraid to break the silence, to break the spell,

His lips had parted a little now, she could see the tongue move across the stained teeth. But his eyes remained closed, and there was something so distant about his face that it seemed he was not there at all. How could she make an objection to someone who was not there to hear her?

Then, in one smooth motion, he drew the zipper all the

way down, grasped her hands and thrust them inside the opening.

Ellen gasped. Her hands fumbled against hot hairy skin, the round hard shaft lying against the belly.

"No, like this," he muttered, from his distant, apparently sleeping face, and he took her fingers and curled them around that throbbing trunk of flesh, and moved them up and down, up and down.

Ellen struggled in confusion. He had stolen words from her, he had stolen true perception and will. Yet she knew what her hands felt — the skin moving loosely on the shaft, his buttocks subtly writhing. She heard his breath sputtering out through his lips. He was pretending with his face that nothing was happening.

She was frightened and repelled, but his face said, Nothing is happening, Absolutely nothing unusual is happening, while his short fingers gripped hers, pumping them up and down, up and down on his penis that stood up against his hairy belly like something that lived an independent life.

Then he gave a low "Unnnnnnnnh" — and his hands held hers still. She felt a pulsing in the flesh under her fingers and saw the whitish fluid spurt out the end and spread sticky and thick on the belly.

She looked up at Zangaro's face. It was blotched with dark color, the lips shone wet. But the eyes remained closed, and there was no expression but his usual stern scornful one.

Then his hands lifted carefully from hers, and she pulled her fingers away, unwinding them from the shaft of flesh that had become soft and fell to the side. She drew her hands back into her lap and sat there in amazement and shame. Her body was terribly hot, all her clothes constricting it. Her breath was shallow. Never before in her seventeen years had she seen a man's genitals. Her brothers and her father kept theirs discreetly hidden. Once when she had danced close with a boy she had felt him get hard down there. That was the extent of her sophistication.

Having zipped his pants, Mr. Zangaro was buckling his belt. Those small clever eyes were finally open, but they wore an expression of studied casualness, and they did not look at Ellen. He turned his chair back to the desk, and lifted the papers there.

Ellen sat watching him, her whole body uneasy. And to escape the sourness rising in her throat, she searched in her mind for some inkling of what would happen now. Glancing at the bed, she thought that what must happen now would be that he would "make love to" her. She had read a novel in which the older man initiated the young woman into sex; he was very gentle and afterwards he looked at her body and told her she was beautiful, and because he said so she knew she was a real woman at last. Was that what was going to happen between her and Zangaro now? Were they having an "affair"? All of this must mean that he loved and wanted her. It must mean that! She struggled to place the fantasy between herself and what she knew.

It was steamy hot and silent in the room, except for the quiet sounds of the papers being moved on the desk.

Zangaro cleared his throat, and Ellen felt the sound in her own body.

"Here," he said, "I think we'd better change this paragraph." He read, "For only $3.50 a session, you can learn the secrets of the most glamorous models . . . uh . . . no, mannequins . . . in the . . . uh . . . dazzling . . . whaddayou think of that, Ellen, dazzling okay? . . . umh . . . in the dazzling world of high fashion." He bent over to write in the changes.

Ellen sat staring at his profile.

Briskly, he stacked the sheets, handed them to her. Her hands were so numb that she let the papers slip to the rug. He waited while she retrieved them. Then he stood up and said, "Mary should be done with the typewriter by now, and you can get started."

He went to the door, opened it, waited for her.

The room had filled with shadow. She sat staring at his figure by the door, could just make out the impatient arch of his eyebrows. Slowly she raised herself from the chair and walked across the room, past the bed, past him, and out into the hall.

When they entered the office downstairs, the secretary glanced up, examining Ellen with a knowing look. Ellen felt herself go scarlet.

"Let her get to work there, when you're finished," Zangaro said, and went off quickly into the back room.

That was so many long years ago. Yet the remembrance is vivid in Ellen — how she had not been able to meet the secretary's eyes. She had stood heavy and miserable, clutching the sheaf of papers, staring at the photographs of sleek women that lined the walls. And that evening, riding home on the bus, filled with self-loathing, she was repulsed by her own hands. She was repulsed by herself.

Now Ellen realizes how far up the beach she has wandered, below the looming cliffs. The man with the dogs is a tiny figure in the mist far behind her. She looks out to where the waves curl and foam in the khaki water. Abruptly she glances up at the cliffs, and sees there the upper body of a man, bent slightly forward, watching her. She stops, and stands looking up. Yes, here where there is no one else, she has become the prey. The man is too high up to be clearly seen. He might as well be Zangaro in the dim room, standing at the door.

Casually, Ellen moves up closer to the cliff, looking about her at the debris strewn on the sand. When she glances up again, his figure is gone, and she stoops to pick up the piece of wood she has spotted. It is a heavy chunk of board, broken off from one of the logs that roll in on the surf. And at its end is a rusty bolt partially embedded.

She chooses a patch of warm sand up near the cliff and sits down facing the sea, putting the piece of wood next to her. Leaning back on stiffened arms, she watches the waves break and smooth out and come sliding up the sand, glimmering silver where the sun hits them.

Ellen is perfectly still inside. She smiles a bitter smile as she remembers how years later she had heard that Zangaro sued his wife for divorce, claiming she was a lesbian. How like him it was. And how wonderfully ironic it would have been if the woman *had* been a lesbian. But Ellen doubts that. More likely it was his own imagination and weird desire that had concocted the story.

She lowers her head to rest on her knees, and tries to listen to the sounds about her, to enter, if only for a few moments, into the natural universe. Under the shoosh of each succeeding wave, is the steady dull roar, like a giant engine. If Ellen were not so familiar with it she might look up to scan the sky, expecting to see a plane. But she knows it is the voice of the ocean, interminably speaking. Recognizing it, she cannot enter it now, for in her head lurks the possibility of what the next few minutes will bring.

It is not long before she begins to hear a scraping and scrambling on the cliff behind her. Her whole body listens as she sees a yellow rock roll down onto the sand.

Then she can feel the presence beside her, and she turns her head to look.

Above shiny brown loafers are neatly pressed wool

trousers, a white shirt and wide tie under a tweed sports jacket. His face is pink and his thick salt-and-pepper eyebrows sit like little caterpillars up high on his forehead. His hair is black with patches of grey in it, stylishly cut, full but not too long, as might befit an appliance salesman or a TV personality. His anxious eyes blink at Ellen.

"Hello," he says brightly, and he reaches down to his fly, which is already open, and pulls out a short uncircumcized cock and fleshy balls, all of an odd pasty color. He holds this soft pile of genitals in the palms of his hands, offering it to Ellen like a doughy bouquet.

She gets quickly to her feet, clutching the piece of wood.

Leaning forward, she shouts into the sea wind. "You must really want to get yourself in trouble, doing that, you must want someone to call the police on you, I could go get them right now, I could bring them back here and they'd find you and lock you up, is that what you want? Is it?"

He stands leaning his shoulders back away from her, his pelvis rocked forward. His pink face is a mask of humiliation.

"No," he says, "I want a woman."

"Oh, really?!" Ellen throws up her hand. "You want a woman. This is how you expect to find a woman?"

"Yes," he says stubbornly.

"You don't want a woman, you just want someone to *look* at you, isn't that right!"

He scrunches his neck down into the collar of his shirt and does not answer. And Ellen realizes that he has been getting what he wanted: she has been looking at him.

Lifting the stick, she takes a threatening step toward him, expecting him to move away from her. But he simply cringes, and his face with its fuzzy eyebrows perched up

75

high has on it an expression that says, I know I am despicable. Whatever you may do to me will not be sufficient to punish me for what I am.

Ellen is stopped. She cannot bear looking into his eyes, which are so deep with self-despising. He makes her experience some part of herself which she does not want to own, and she is held there, bound to him in weakness, disgust.

She drops the piece of wood on the sand. Going around him, she begins to walk toward the parking lot.

"Hey!" he calls softly, but Ellen goes on without looking back, her mind already turning to her house, the friend with whom she lives. She plods away from him down the beach, leaving him with his hands cupped at his crotch, his face obscenely beseeching.

Steven

Kate Inman

"You can't come."

"Why not?"

"Because we don't want you tagging behind. You never keep up."

"And what are you going to do that she'll have to keep up with, may I ask?" Momma always sticks up for me.

"Nothing. Just riding out there mostly. She can never keep up and she might get lost in the dark. Besides, we're going to watch bats and she won't be quiet enough."

My brother's mean. He never lets me go anywhere with him till I give him my best baseball cards. That's not really true. He let me ride out with him to Susan Johnson's farm two weeks ago and that's at least three miles. But that's because he likes her so much he was scared to go alone. I don't know what he's talking about when he says I can't keep up. He's only going out to the golf course to sleep over night and that's not even a mile. I ride right through there on my way to school every day. He just doesn't want me around because he and Jeff are going to do something Momma won't like. I don't know what it is yet but if I go they won't be able to do it because Steven has to be responsible for me. Besides, they think I might tell. No matter how much I tell them I won't tell they still think I'll tell.

"What if I go, too? I'll ride with Janice and you can go on ahead. That way you can watch your bats off in a corner by yourselves and she can go, too. I haven't slept outside in a long time. That might be really nice."

My sister's alright. I like being with her because she doesn't always run off to do special private things like Steven. All I ever hear with him is rushing in my head when I can't breathe fast enough or keep up. It's different with Anna. She tells me to hush and listen to the night noises: spring peepers crying like tiny birds begging for worms, bullfrogs moaning like cows, like Momma blowing on her empty beer bottle. One night in the woods we sat still for so long a raccoon came out of the trees on the other side of the stream and started fishing in the moonlight. It splattered little ripples of silver on the silver fish and over the water to us sitting on a rock on the other side. It's different with Anna.

We've got our sleeping bags ready now. I have to tie mine on because my baskets aren't as big as Steven's or Anna's.

"Janice, do you have a pillow?" Momma always asks if I have a pillow.

"No, I'll use my jacket."

"Why don't you take a pillow. You know you always end up using someone else's." But I don't want a pillow. It just means one more thing to carry when we get off our bikes.

Riding now, we have to watch out for the three trees in the middle of our street. They haven't put a street light up at our corner yet so we can't see well enough sometimes when the moon isn't out. Now there's half and I can see the road disappear in two shadows on either side of the first tree. I ride close behind Anna because she knows the pot holes better than I do in the dark.

I try to remember why I run after Steven all the time. Every time I do I feel hot and mad. It's almost like he does things on purpose to make me mad like riding faster than I can keep up or going to a baseball game where he said he'd take me when he knows I still have chores to do. With Anna I feel quiet and good. I decide that the next time Steven rides off fast I'm not even going to try keeping up with him.

The golf course is at the bottom end of town sloping down to the woods and creek bed. There aren't any lights except at the edges near the houses, theatre, and tennis courts, and one on a tree near the bike path that runs through the middle to my school. On the uphill side towards town there is a baseball diamond with a row of three or four trees next to it where we have agreed to meet and decide from there where to sleep. Steven and Jeff are there ahead of me and Anna talking in whispers and looking at something with their flashlights. They shove whatever it is in their pockets when we walk our bikes up to them through the wet grass.

"It took you long enough, where've you been?" I want to punch him but Anna speaks.

"Just where you've been only slower. Where do you want to sleep?"

We drag our bikes down into a place where the gound makes a little valley with lights from town hidden by the upper hillside. Steven and Jeff leave their bikes with ours and take their sleeping bags off to watch bats behind a bump in the ground circling one side of a green. They want to go further but Anna tells them to stay within yelling distance in case we get cold and decide to go home or I start throwing up my dinner like I did the time at Piedmont Lake when I ate too many marshmallows. We all know that's not going to happen because all I ate for dinner was pork chops and mashed potatoes which I never throw up, but Anna insists anyway.

I lay my bag out on even ground and crawl in with my

clothes on to look at the starts. Anna lays her bag next to mine but sits awhile looking off towards the woods. I can see her, black against the light from the houses that comes in streaks over our heads from behind the hill. She looks calm. I always wonder what she's thinking when she looks like that and I try to find out in a way she won't think I'm guessing.

"What do you think Steven and Jeff are doing now?"

"Watching bats, what do you think?"

"I don't know but I bet they aren't watching bats. I bet they're doing something with whatever they were looking at when we came up. What do you think it was?"

"Pictures of girls."

I start. Her voice is harsh and impatient like it is when she's tired of waiting for Steven to stop acting crummy. I've never heard her sound that disgusted. I almost forget what to say next.

"How do you know?"

"Because I saw them in Steven's room this morning when I emptied his wastebasket and I saw him put them in his pocket tonight before we left."

Now I really don't know what to say. I want to ask her more but I suddenly remember what I forgot this morning: that I was supposed to empty the wastebaskets and didn't. If I'd done it then I would have seen, not Anna. I wouldn't have to ask anything and she wouldn't know to sound so disgusted.

I can see from the way she's sitting that she's mad at something. She's sitting straighter and tighter than before. If I saw her face I bet she'd be frowning like she does when Steven starts swearing only worse. The pictures must be like the one I caught Steven looking at under the table at dinner once and made him show me afterwards. It was of a woman all dressed up in shiny clothes with lots of lipstick and make-up on. She had one foot up on a stool and she looked like she was taking off her stockings. Steven made a face at me when he gave it to me and I had this funny tingly feeling in my stomach when he did like it had something to do with me.

Anna is still sitting tight, staring off towards the trees. Her breath is puffy, making clouds out of her mouth. I want to say something to her but I don't know what. My face gets hot instead. I make clouds with my breath next to hers and listen to the night noises from the woods. I can hear a tree toad far away, like music in outer space. Somewhere there's a green frog burping like a washtub base but not from the woods.

From the tennis courts, voices coming closer, men's voices burping and rough like new cut wood, sometimes raising like a buzzsaw laughing heavy dry heaves, then lowering into murky simmering burps. Anna jumps up into the stream of light washing from the houses near the tennis courts, then crouches low hitting me down when I try to get out of my sleeping bag and stand up.

"Who are they? What's . . . "

"Sssshhh!"

Her hand on my arm, my body tense, eyes straining to catch shadows playing across the stream of light above our heads. I can feel my ankle grinding into the zipper of my sleeping bag and I try to move a little but Anna's hand tightens on my arm. I freeze clutching the sleeping bag and my foot.

"What d'you thing it was anyway, a rabbit? Hell! It's so fukkin' dark out here you could run into a tree as easy as not. Yer so drunk anyway you wouldn't know what hit ya."

"What d'ya mean? I ain't drunk, yer drunk. And I swear

it was a girl popped up right over there. Come on, it would-
n't hurt nothin' to look . . . "

Their voices lower, burping together like telling secrets,
rasping and coming closer till we see their shadows in the
light above us. Anna grips my arm harder, almost hurting.
She waves her hand at me like she wants me to stay or go
back somewhere, then she's gone up in the light walking
towards the shadows.

I feel the ground pounding under me, the wet grass like
little hands holding me tight. She is up there somewhere in
the light walking towards the voices through the grass that
doesn't hold her back. *In a room so white I can't see, waiting, with men in white, voices low and murmuring at the
other end. One breaks off, comes over to me, speaks: Your
mother is going away, she's going to the hospital and you
won't see her for awhile. We don't allow children under
twelve to visit in the hospital but we promise to take good
care of her so she can come home soon. Don't worry, we'll
take care of everything.*

*Momma. They're taking Momma away. The men are
taking her away and they won't let me see her again. Momma
Momma don't go Momma, don't go Anna,* walking up in
the light towards the voices towards the men *Anna don't go,
they'll take you away, they'll take you away and I'll never
see you again Anna run Anna get away, run Anna run!*
Bursting my chest my arms my legs my eyes bursting hot
breath and tears into the light, for a moment caught like
crystal I see black figures bunched against the light sucking
in another figure half turned flowing hair screaming *Steven
Steven* as she falls to the ground, my head bursting lights
from behind them bursting into the shadows through the
shadows, kicking scratching biting everything I can get my
feet my hands my mouth on screaming *don't touch, don't
touch, don't take her away!* Pounding, deep voices rasping

close, rasping hairy hands clawing me away, reaching for my face my eyes, clutching my hair, hot stinky breath stronger than beer rushing over my face, *get them out get them away, pound them pound them.* Anna, warm Anna holds me back crying tears and voice crying *Janice Janice stop it Janice stop.* Somewhere in the dark Steven slides in between, jabbing back and forth, Jeff hanging back, Steven hitting shadows, hanging back, yelling *leave her alone you fuck off and leave her alone or else* . . . the men's heavy roar drowning closer hanging shadows over our heads, over Anna screaming *run Steven, Jeff, run Janice RUN!*

I remember riding back, tears pouring down, shaking so bad I could hardly keep my bike on the road. I didn't even notice that we'd left our flashlights with our sleeping bags when we ran. I remember dumping my bike on the terrace, running in the side door left unlocked just in case, running *like once before running past a Black woman ironing our clothes, hired while my mother is gone,* running down the hall to her room *only now it's dark, it's night out this time* as I fling myself crying *like once before* half onto her bed, my hands reaching around her just wakening shape, crying *like before,* "Momma Momma you're home Momma, I'm home, we're home Momma," tears settling into the quiet of her arms.

We had a big feast the next night and I got to sit at the head of the table. Everyone laughed and looked at each other funny when I told them I thought the men were taking Anna away. Momma said they'd have hurt her a lot but they wouldn't have taken her away. Anna kept squeezing my hand and smiling at me but she looked sad and a little sick the way Momma did when Grandma died. I kept wanting to tell her everything was OK and to be happy because she didn't get hurt and nobody died but I didn't know how to say it so I just smiled back at her a lot and talked more.

Steven was quiet when he laughed with the others, he didn't sneer like he usually does. He doesn't sneer or make faces at me at all anymore. He's quieter and a lot nicer. He lets me go with him to baseball games now and doesn't seem to mind when I'm there. Sometimes he helps me fix my bike and even teaches me the parts I don't know. He used to get mad when I didn't know exactly how to grease the bearings or adjust the brakes. He used to grab my bike and say, "Here, let me do it." Now he tells me what to do and lets me do it myself. He watches while I do it.

I don't feel so rushed to keep up with him anymore. I can't figure out what happened but he's been like that ever since the night on the golf course. Sometimes I catch him looking funny at Anna like he's worried about her, like he's afraid she might go away. Sometimes I even catch him watching me like he doesn't understand. He looks away quick when he sees me notice.

I asked Momma about him one day. I said, "What's wrong with Steven? He's a lot nicer than he used to be."

"There's nothing wrong with him, he's just changing. He's growing up."

"Do you think I'll like him when he's all grown up?"

"I don't know. Do you like him now?"

"I like him a lot better now than I did before but if he keeps changing how do I know he won't change into somebody I don't like again?"

"I guess you don't know."

— *for my brother*

The Grandchild

Evan Rubin

If it makes a difference, I really was a good child the whole week before Grandma Yettle died. I didn't aggravate my father because he had enough on his mind. I didn't ask any of my stupid questions about Grandma Yettle or Grandpa Baruch. I especially didn't ask anything about the boxes or the mirrors. I took care of myself after school so my mother could stay with my father at Grandma Yettle's rest home. I fed Erica, our Airedale who was only a year old then. I picked up my room without waiting to be told. And although it doesn't matter, for almost a week, I wished as hard as I could for my grandmother not to die. It was only that very last day that was terrible.

I came home from school and let myself in with my own key. Each day that Grandma Yettle was sick, my mother left a letter for me tacked to the refrigerator door with a magnet. So first things first, I went to the kitchen to read the letter. There are nectarines in the fruit bowl, the letter said, and a good movie on channel seven at three o'clock. I should change my clothes and feed the dog and put the air conditioner on if it's too warm. The letter said my mother would be home at five and I should be sure to have a snack because we wouldn't meet my father for dinner, in a restaurant, until late. And p.s., there's Danish in the bread box.

Of course, I knew everything the letter told me. I knew where the nectarines were and how to look up a movie in the *T.V. Guide.* In fact, I knew more then this. I knew what order to do everything in. I knew I should change my clothes first because there's no point to wearing good clothes around the house. I knew to feed Erica before I had my own snack because a hungry animal shouldn't have to watch his master eat. I even knew that Grandma Yettle might die, although no one had told me this exactly. I knew she might die while I was watching the television.

Grandma Yettle was very sick and I should try to be good. She was very sick because she was very old and her arteries had hardened. She had lived a long life and now her body was wearing out. Her arteries had hardened and her blood just creeped along. When an old person is very sick, my mother explained, the grandchildren, unless they're old enough to be married, stay at home and try to be good. Do the grandchildren go to the funeral? I didn't dare ask. Do the grandchildren sit on boxes? If Grandma died, where would we get the boxes? From the Rabbi? From the funeral parlor? Would they bring Grandma Yettle to our house, dead in a box? Maybe that was the box we were supposed to sit on. Why don't people send flowers to Jews?

I didn't watch the movie that day. I went to the family room and took the photograph album out of the book case. Finding the picture of Grandma Yettle was easy. It was in with the others from my last birthday party. My father had picked Grandma Yettle up at the rest home so she could come to my party. My mother explained to me that it was a mitzvah for Grandma Yettle to be at my party and it was a mitzvah for me to kiss her because she was very old.

In the picture, Grandma Yettle was standing with her hands on my cousin Cindy's shoulders and I think that was a mitzvah, too. Grandma Yettle didn't look ignorant, she just looked old. Her hair looked like cotton candy when it's almost gone, when just a tiny bit of pink fuzz is left on the white cardboard cone. Of course, her hair wasn't pink. It was greyish brown, the color of dust. And her skin wasn't white, either. It was Jewish colored and it was coming loose. I remember when I kissed her on my birthday, I was afraid of tearing her old face on one of its seams. I don't think she understood that it was my birthday that day. She didn't understand very much at all, partly because she was already old and sick and her arteries had begun to harden, and partly because Grandma Yettle was an ignorant woman.

When my father was a young child, Grandma Yettle was so ignorant she didn't use scissors. When my father's fingernails grew too long, Grandma Yettle would bite them off with her teeth. Once, she tore one of his nails right off, and to this day, that nail grows in crooked, almost sideways. My father calls that finger his bird finger, and it has magical powers. If I wasn't good, my father would wave his bird finger at me. I'd better watch out, he would say, or I might fall under the spell of the bird finger.

I used to ask my father questions about Grandma Yettle. How come she was too ignorant to know about scissors? I knew about scissors and I was only a child. I even had my own scissors and I could cut out a picture from a magazine so that no white would show around the edges. If I needed to use scissors with pointed ends, for making holes, I was allowed to use the scissors that were kept in the drawer in the kitchen. There were also little manicure scissors in the bathroom cabinet. No one in my family would use their teeth. Dad, I'd ask, how come Grandma Yettle used her teeth?

"Because she's an ignorant woman."

"Does she still use her teeth?"

"No. Now she uses her gums."

"What's an ignorant woman, anyhow?" Was my mother an ignorant woman? What are ignorant women like when they're children?

"She's just an ignorant woman. That's all." Sometimes I could make my father mad by asking too many questions.

"Can she read?"

"No. She can't read or write. She's an ignorant woman."

"Why can't she read or write?"

"Because she's ignorant. Now leave me alone. If you're so interested in genealogy, go ask your mother about her family."

"What's that?"

"What's what?"

"Genealogy."

"It's something for Protestants."

"Protestants? Is Mother Protestant?" It couldn't be.

"No, but the way she talks about her family, you'd think they came over on the Mayflower."

"What was the name of the boat Grandma Yettle came over on?"

"Don't you ever run out of questions?"

"Was Grandpa Baruch on the same boat as Grandma Yettle?"

"Do you ask your teacher this many questions?"

"What was he like anyhow?"

"Who?"

"Grandpa Baruch. Was he an ignorant man?"

"Him? They hung him for stealing a rope."

"Stealing a rope?" I already knew this joke, but I went along with it.

"Yea, stealing a rope." My father would pretend to be serious. "Yea. There was a horse at the end of it." Then we'd both laugh and he'd tell me if I didn't leave him alone he'd get me with his bird finger.

The truth is, Grandpa Baruch sold fruit. My mother told me.

"Sold fruit? You mean in a supermarket?"

"No. On a corner."

"On a corner? Like that guy we saw with the monkey? Did Grandpa Baruch have a monkey?"

"No. He had a pushcart. Italians have monkeys. Jews have pushcarts. It's nothing to be shamed of."

I had a thousand more questions. "Why was Grandma Yettle an ignorant woman?"

"Because she worked all day long in a sweat shop and didn't have time to learn anything."

A sweat shop! Now I was getting someplace. I already knew about the sweat shops. "Did Grandma Yettle's sweat shop ever catch on fire?" Grandma Ida's sweat shop caught on fire and burned to the ground. All the women ran to the door but even the door was on fire and most of them couldn't escape. There were no windows to jump from because the men who owned the sweat shop didn't want the women to look outside when they were supposed to be working. It was a famous fire and Grandma Ida was one of the lucky ones who lived to tell about it. There were even stories about the fire in the front page of the newspaper. Was Grandma Ida's picture in the paper?

Oh what am I thinking about Grandma Ida for? She's

not going to die. I was supposed to be thinking about Grandma Yettle. Why do my thoughts keep wandering? I had to concentrate.

I took the picture of Grandma Yettle and my cousin Cindy and held it very close to my face with both hands so I couldn't see anything else. I covered my cousin Cindy with my thumb so all I could see was Grandma Yettle. I was ready to concentrate. Don't die yet, Grandma Yettle. I said it with all the powers of my mind. Don't die. Don't die. Don't die yet, Grandma Yettle. Don't die and make my father tear his clothes. If you died, would I have to cover the mirror in my room? Is it bad luck to cover a mirror? Oh please don't die yet, Grandma Yettle. Don't die. Don't die until I'm older. Don't die, Grandma Yettle. Don't die.

Just as I was beginning to use all my mental powers, a dog barked outside. This might seem like a small interruption when one is really concentrating, but the barking outside triggered Erica inside. Erica started barking, too, and ran to the front door.

When I got to the door, I stopped. I put one hand on Erica's head and one hand on her tail and I told her that before I let her out, we would do a seance mitzvah for Grandma Yettle. Erica was an unusually smart dog, even for an Airedale, and they tend to be an intelligent breed. In fact, the day Grandma Yettle came to my birthday party, my mother said, "She knows," meaning Erica. Good little Erica kissed Grandma Yettle's hands very gently instead of jumping all over her, which might have knocked her down and made her pass away right there and then.

"Erica," I said, "we've got to put all our powers together and command Grandma Yettle not to die."

But Erica didn't want to. She pulled away and whined at the door. "Oh go on out, you stupid dog." I opened the door and Erica dashed toward a big strange dog who must have been the dog who started all the barking. I'd never seen that dog before and I wish Erica and I had never seen him at all.

I went back to the family room and picked up the picture. There was no time to waste. I put the picture in the center of the floor, face up. I would walk around the picture seven times and each time around, I would say, "Don't die, Grandma Yettle," three times. Or maybe I should do it three times, saying seven Don't Die's. I decided to do it once each way. No, I would have to do it three times each way, or seven times each way. Only three's and seven's would work. I was on my second time around when I heard Erica scream.

I'd never heard her voice like that. I ran to the door and out of the house. It was a dog fight!

Poor Erica's little beige body and the black and brown body of that strange dog were mixed up together in a spinning ball that growled and tumbled over itself along the edge of our lawn. They were so tangled and tumbling so fast I could hardly tell one dog from the other. I knew Erica's neck could be broken or one of her legs ripped off. Oh Erica! I ran to save her faster then I ever thought I could run. When I tried to grab her, I fell into the spinning wheel of dogs. One of us shrieked, it could have been any of the three of us, and it was over. I don't know what happened to the big dog, but Erica ran straight for the front door and I did too.

Erica didn't stop running until she got to the far corner of the living room. She was crying and her little stump of a tail looked like it was just glued to her behind. Oh Erica, don't be frightened. I put my face on her neck. She jerked away and I saw her eye.

Her eye, her right eye, in the inside corner, where it was supposed to be white, was deep red. That dirty dog cut Erica's eye. I held my breath and waited for the gush of blood. I waited for the blood to pour out from that cut, pour and pour down Erica's cheek, down her nose, down her chest, pour and pour until she was covered with blood and her eyeball finally collapsed. I waited but no blood came.

Was she blind? Don't be blind, Erica. I waved my arm on an arch across my body. Erica's head followed my motion. But her sense of smell could have told her how my arm was moving. Could she see me? I had to devise a better test.

I walked into the kitchen. Erica followed but that didn't mean anything. She could tell where I was going by the sound of my feet. I went to the cupboard and took out a dog biscuit. Erica jumped around like she always does when someone has a biscuit. She still had her appetite. That was a good sign. I told her to sit, to stay. But she wouldn't calm down. It must be the pain from her eye. I told her firmly, "Stay, Erica!" and walked to the other end of the kitchen. She was right at my heels. For the test to work, I had to get far enough away from her so she couldn't smell the biscuit.

Finally, I struck upon an idea. I moved a chair next to the sink and climbed up. I was standing on the kitchen counter. I put both hands behind my back and switched the biscuit from hand to hand. Erica had her front paws up on the chair. She was trying to climb up too. Erica, watch. I put both arms out like Jesus on the cross, with the biscuit in one hand and the other hand empty. Which hand, Erica? Can you see the biscuit?

Erica started to cry. Oh, she knows she's blind. I climbed down from the counter to the chair and from the chair to the floor. I hugged Erica and she snatched the biscuit right out of my hand. Did she see the biscuit? Could she still see? Maybe it was the smell. Or maybe she could still see in her good eye. I hadn't thought of that. But if the cut made her blind in one eye, it wouldn't be long before the other eye went blind too. That always happens when one eye goes blind.

While Erica was eating the biscuit, I bent down to examine her cut. Had it become bigger and redder? Was it really spreading?

I heard the front door open and my mother's voice called, "Hello." As fast as I could I told my mother what happened, about the big dog I'd never seen before, how I didn't mean for Erica to get hurt, how she might be blind, how it wasn't exactly bleeding but was cut. My mother put her purse down and checked Erica over very carefully.

"Oh poor little Erica," was the first thing she said. She rubbed the dog behind her ears.

"Is she going to die?"

"No. Don't be silly." My mother laughed at me. "It's nothing. It's just a scratch."

"Is she blind?"

"No. Of course not. It's nothing at all. It's superficial. It probably didn't even hurt her. It's nothing to worry about."

"What's superficial?"

"The cut."

"No. What's it mean?"

"It means it's on the outside, not in the inside. In a few days you won't even be able to see it. But if you want, we can have the vet look at her tomorrow."

"No." By tomorrow, it might be in the inside. "It's nothing."

"What's this chair doing here?" My mother pushed the chair away from the counter and back under the table.

I couldn't tell her. "Oh, nothing."

"Well, it must be doing something here." My mother opened the cabinet above the counter, directly above where the chair was. On the bottom shelf were cans, soup cans, vegetable cans, gravy cans. On the top shelf were the liquor bottles for company. "Now what was the chair doing here?"

"I wanted to look out of the window." I told a lie. There was a window above the sink. My mother didn't ask me anything else about the chair.

"Did you watch the movie?"

"No."

"What did you do all afternoon?"

"Oh, nothing much."

My mother kissed me on the chin and went to change her clothes. Everyone in my family changes their clothes when they come home. There's no point in wearing good clothes around the house. I stayed in the kitchen with Erica.

Maybe the cut wasn't superficial. Maybe the reason it wasn't bleeding on the outside was because it was bleeding on the inside. Maybe her whole eyeball had already turned to blood except for the outside shell. Maybe the arteries that connect her eyeballs to her brain were softening and turning to blood. And her brain. Maybe the cut had already spread so far that her brain was melting, becoming slushier and soupier until the whole inside of her head was just liquid blood.

Erica lay under the table. She was perfectly still. Her eyes were closed. She was dying. My mouth was perfectly dry. My stomach had gone into my throat to drain off my spit, which is what it always does whenever something terrible is ready to happen. Erica was going to pass away.

Oh Erica, you can't. You just can't die. I'd miss you so much. I'd never want to do anything again. Oh Erica, don't die. I had to concentrate. I had to use all my powers to command Erica again and again and again until it worked. I crawled under the table and put my hand on Erica's head. Don't die, Erica. Don't pass away and don't die. Don't die, Erica.

Oh why had I wasted my three's and seven's on Grandma Yettle? Why had I used up all of my mental powers on her when I needed it now for Erica? Oh why had I given my solemn promise to always be good if only Grandma Yettle wouldn't die? I had used up everything and now I had nothing left to save my dog. I tried again and again to concentrate but it was no use.

I knew what I had to do. It was a terrible thing to do but I would rather sit on boxes for a year than have Erica die. I would rather cover every mirror in the house than have Erica die. I would rather have anything happen. I closed my eyes and this time I was able to concentrate.

I take it back. I take it back. I take it all back from Grandma Yettle. I take it back, everything I said. You can die now, Grandma Yettle. You don't have to wait until I'm older. I take back everything I said before. I take it all back from Grandma Yettle and put it all into Erica.

My mother called me from the family room. When I went to see what she wanted I saw her standing in the middle of the room with the picture of Grandma Yettle and my cousin Cindy. "What was this picture doing on the floor?"

My face became so hot it burned. "Nothing."

My mother told me it must be doing something and asked me if I was worried about Grandma Yettle. I didn't say anything. My mother told me I was a very good child. My face burned so much it sizzled. I knew I was a wicked child.

The telephone rang. My mother was still looking at me when she picked up the phone. Her voice was soft. "Oh darling, I'm so sorry . . . . I'm sorry I wasn't with you . . . . Shall I come get you? . . . . Are you alright to drive? . . . . We should thank God she didn't have to suffer any longer than she did . . . . " My mother hung up the phone and put her arms around me.

"Honey, that was Daddy."

"I know." Yes, I knew. Grandma Yettle was dead. Tears started streaming out my eyes. I didn't mean to cry but I was crying. And not just with my eyes. My lungs were heaving up and down. I was crying very hard and I couldn't stop.

"You know, sometimes when an old person dies," my mother said, "it's really a blessing in disguise."

Out of nowhere, Erica was there at our feet, jumping around so much you'd think we had all the dog biscuits in the world hidden in our pockets. I freed myself from my mother and bent down to Erica.

The cut on her eye was getting smaller. Yes, my mother was right. Sometimes when an old person dies, it's a blessing in disguise.

In Memoriam:
Carolyn Johnson

Chris Llewellyn

Carolyn Johnson:

you died two weeks ago.

I am the secretary

sent to take your place.

Your glasses and cupcakes

are still in your desk

and I write this

with your pen.

I am angry at your life.

I am angry at your death.

One workday I saw you

fifty shakey smokin toomuch

too overweight too lonely.

And I am too angry

at your life.

One afternoon you left

the office Alone you went

home Alone and

died Alone

in your Apartment.

It was two days before they

found you filed under A

(Alone).

I've finished transcribing and

typed final copy from your drafts.

Carolyn Johnson:

Who says women

can't be drafted?

Cause we're all drafts —

incomplete roughcopy

onionskin foolscap

manifold carboncopy

throwaway getanother

tissuetypewriter

womansecretary

officewife.

I take a clean sheet

rollit in the carriage

and center your name:

    Carolyn Johnson.

Then rollit up and smoke it

cause Carol I'm all keyedup

and I feel it in my bonds

in my tissues in my

correctype liquidpaper brain.

Say after breathin whiteout

mimeofluid typecleaner

thirty (30) years were you

hi when you died?

Glad you were cremated

not filed ina drawer under

watermarked engraved letterhead:

Carolyn Johnson.

Stop.

Reachout fingers on homerows

deathrows of the world &

touch home touch my face touch

Carolyn's ashes somewhere in

Pennsylvania touch away

machinated lives mere extensions

of machines clicking tapping

thudding tiny nails in coffin lids

ticking clocks in mausoleumed

officebuildings and deliver us

from margins comma cleartabs

capitalize your periods don't reset

space bar lock shift index return

return

return

return:

Carolyn Johnson.

Susie Q

Red Arobateau

1.

She breezed into the club with a strong rap. Television was into womens lib & it was a new day. Women was tired of giving up their money to a nigger. A ho was no longer a bitch.

The bar was filled with white hippies. Walls painted black, and red lamps along the sides. A horse-shoe shaped bar that someone had thrown together up front, dancefloor behind it. Tables and chairs along the wall. Suzie thought how much it looked like Pappys which had hos lined up gabbing or nodding out leaning up against the counter where fried chicken and softdrinks was for sale, when they should be out on the curb working. Nothing but women on the barstools; black and red shadows cast on their faces that were boyish smooth & hairless. But there was a difference. These women here were lesbians.

She was a character with the appearance of mini mouse. Skinny legs. Her shoes too big for her feet.—She'd bought 'em, now she'd have to wear 'em. Bronze complexion, her hair cornrowed—at ten cents a braid down at the Kings & Queens Beauty Saloon—but hiding under a wig that sat on her like a hat. Full lips, big round eyes with a hardened look that she could turn on or off. Of medium height—5'5" and weight, 130 pounds well porportioned on her frame. Not an extra ounce of fat from all that walking & standing. Her spirits are exuberent tonight. A party mood. Body full of energy—that came from her mind, for physically she was worn out. Suzie had on a tiny little outfit pink, showing a big expanse of bare copper colored skin on arms & legs that bore plenty of bruises. Scars darker then others, some fresh bluish marks.

She had got to the club—half way 'cross town by showing the busdriver an old transfer she'd found in the street. The first bus she'd got on the driver had read it and told her: "THIS IS NO GOOD LADY." Suzie yelled back: "DID IT COME OUT YO' POCKET?" Dismounted, walked 5 blocks, tried another bus, and as she'd sashayed down the aysle weary, in a world-wise-manner, the driver didn't have enough nerve to call her back & demand she feed the fare box those precious coins.

A bedraggled pheasant, she walked in the door, her plumage dragging. 'The only reason why I come back here wuz we *pahteed* last time we wuz here. Folks get down, girl, with wistles & bells & tamboreenes, and they *dannnce!*'

Of course that was the only reason for being here that she'd admit.

On the busride she'd seen out the window black youths do Kung Fu like alley cats leaping into thin air, backs arched. And she made a mental note to herself 'that's the next thang, soon as I get my place, get my kids, I'm gonna learn Karate, & I'll chop a niggers head off if he mess with me one more time.'

Red & black lights revolved, her brain spun. Sleepless too many nights. The wig sat listlessly on her head. The bar curved away from her into the distance, as if embracing the cashregister. Not but a few women, holding conversations in low tones. Monday, it was an off night. A high ceiling, and long the bar echoed with notes from a jukebox. 'Last time I wuz here they had a live band. Guess 'cause it's Monday. . .but that's cool.'

103

Suzie was not too smart, but very verbose. A meger intelligence had been allotted to her, plus no education going for her. In addition, she's young and hasn't gained wisdom. But it don't stop her, not one bit! Talkative. One white woman, the sophisticated kind has come up; despite that $40 like the skins of frogs—green, slippery against her thigh, tucked in the top of her stockings, Suzie tells the woman, "Buy me a drank, I'm broke." And her eyes, a moment ago wide, staring into space as she jiggled her legs and tapped her nails on the bar, her look immediately hardens. "Ain't got a cent, it's the end of the month," she adds. "Oh really?" Says the woman looking directly in her eyes. She's overweight, older in her 40's and has a pantsuit over her pearshaped body, and a friendly smile on her face. Gives the young woman a knowing look. Suzie's strong hustling rap won't get over too swell here. It wasn't necessary, and most women can see thru it.

The lady buys her a drink. Soon the two are rapping. Words spill out Suzies mouth one after another. A little wad of white stuff is in the cornor of her mouth, not wiped away and her eyes glazed,—from not eating or sleeping. The woman asks her if she'd like to dance. "*NO.* My body hurts. I'm fuccccccked up."

She gives up on trying to view the woman as a trick. Tho she may never abandon the hustle that she's developed over the last 5 years—thru necessity, Suzie is not as cold hearted as she might seem at first.

She talks about her life, her kids, her man, and why she's here. The woman nods solomnly. After a couple of drinks in the all-women bar, which is still empty—its early, just 10pm, when the red lights are revolving over the barflys like goldfish in a bowl. "Your body is beautiful." The woman says with a knowing twinkle. And touches her arm briefly. Suzie nods, "Right on." She says nodding like

she's a million miles away; "but no touching please."
"I'm sorry." The woman says, modestly. "That's allright—
I know you don't know any better." Suzie says, chin in
the air. —She can't stand for people to touch her—unless
she's getting paid for it.

Down the bar at one end of its magnetends, two women
are throwing the dice cups. "A HORSE ON YOU." One
yells.

Finally the woman leaves. She has to be at work at the
office 9 the next morning. "TAKE CARE OF YOUR
BODY!" She calls out in a friendly tone, and waves good
by.

"I will, I'm number one." Suzie says, but no one hears
her, and the woman is gone out the door.

Red & black shadows play up the walls for her to watch—
nothing else much is happening. Relaxing in a stretch of
bar all to herself—empty stools on both sides, full lips
touch the rim of her glass, the beverage is almost gone,
soon she'll have to worry about getting the next drink,
but those green bucks in her stocking she will preserve
to the bitter end.

One arm stretches to her purse a few inches away on
the wet-stained bar. Bruises on the warm brown flesh;
she retrieves a ciggaret, snaps her lighter. 'No more, I'm
gonna learn Karate, Kung Fu, K-nife & K-razor. . and
K-gun. Shiet."

All thoughts of womens liberation are out. —There were
still many obsticals so many miles high & wide. She's just
trying to survive number one. Get her a little money together and get her own place & get her kids back from her
mothers. This was her struggle. She wished it was less real &
mo' fantasy, like a Micky Mouse cartoon where the villen

gets WHOOPED over the head with a board. But this female liberation like drops of water one by one was beginning to touch her life with information; beginning with the pussy between her own legs, it's as real as life & death. Stark as a heart-attack.

Flash.—It was always him first, never her. And she was sick of being in the life, already. Tired of a backstreet reputation and a sordid existance.

The Good News of liberation had begun to attack this sistahs brain with doubts as to her present profession.

The stop watch in her life. The second glimpse at herself. She was about to move into a new dimension.

In 1977, women were devided.

2.

"My kids are first. They come first. My kids. I got two, a girl 6, the boy, 4. They're number one. I getting my apartment and get my kids back." She tells the bartender vehemently. The bartender agrees and she moves on down the line filling glasses. Suzies thick lips close together—lipstick is wearing off, & her brown eyes stare into the pit of sleeplessness inside her brain.

"When I left Flash Gordon he was sitting there in nothing but his fur-lined hat with his hair in rollers underneeth. Pectoral muscles in his big brown chest, curly hair dissapearing down his stomach in an arrow pointing right at the only thing he's got that's worth anything—his dick. Big brown feets on the shag rug, & a mean expression on his face.

Now don't get me wrong, Flash Gorden is not the kids father. I just chose Flash last month.

I'm in the life."

The clock moved swiftly towards 12 midnight.

3.

No cars were out in front of the club. Gaps of parking places. Next door to a shoddy hotel. Bottles once filled with wine along the gutters can be seen in the empty spaces. But, by 12:30, inside was a little party happening. Bright colors of pantssuits & evening gowns. Folks blowing whistles. You see, welfare folks own no cars. And this monday was the 30th, Mothers Day, so quite a little crowd had arrived.

A butch came to the bar. Brown hair in a short natural, spiffily attired in jacket and pants to match plus vest. Platform shoes on her small feet that elevated her to 5'5" tall. Her brown face held no outword sign of the emotions within her, cooly she strode to the bar.

When she bought her first beverage of the evening—a Coca Cola dyed pink in a tall glass, with it came a napkin and a note that read:

FOR YOUR OWN PROTECTION PLEASE END YOUR CONVERSATIONS INSIDE THE BAR AND NOT OUT IN FRONT OF THE BAR AFTER 2:00 OR YOU WILL BE ARRESTED. SO BE FOREWARNED, IT'S FOR YOUR OWN PROTECTION.

The police had been cracking down on the club—they considered it a dive—but, anybody could see, as the black & red lights danced their reys over the revelers who lept into the air like gazelles, it was not nothing bad going on here, it just bes a party!

The stud sat down at the bar—after debating wether or not to occupy a booth. But you can't meet anybody that way. Slid onto the barstool with the weariness in her bones

of a nigger. —That perpetual wearyness of baring up under
stress. Lots of extra problems of homosexuals; she looked
around to see what they bes into, these others like her.
'If I had a daughter I would name her Gamine. It means
plucky. Ability to stick it out. To endure hardships or
humiliation without complaint.'

The butch sat, elbows on the bar & a hat sat on her head,
her feminine features; a corsage on her lapel, & the rest
of her in the masculine-woman suit, vest, double breasted
jacket & two-toned platform shoes.

Red lamps shone from the bar, streeked her face with
colors. Let us share the butches secret thoughts: Hungry
for a woman, to press her heart against. Chest to chest as
if pressing the love from her heart into the womans heart.
The womans naked body under her own—spreading her
legs. The butch goes down, licking her; the tip of her tongue
flicking, probing, gently pushing the folds of the labia
back with her fingers. Smooth, grainy, that female smell
in her nostrils, mouth sucking, tongue alternately seeking
out that hood shaped spot, and the pearl emerges. — The
fem's clitorus becomes hard. The butches tongue moving
faster, harder in that most loving of physical acts. The
femme moans as she lays back on the bed, her body goes
taut, fingers alternately grasping the butches hair, and the
sheet of the bed at either side. The butch alternately sucks
& licks the womans vagina, concentrating on the clitorus,
then the woman puts her whole mouth against her womans
sex, sucking, while reaching up and fondles her breasts
at the same time. The smell of their own strong sexuality.
Then her mouth pulls away while her hand reaches down
to manipulate the pearl tongue between the womans legs,
while mouth sucking the nipple of one breast and wraping
her arms around her body to play with the womans other

108

nipple. Gently she push her fingers into her mates pussy,
thrusting a little ways, one finger in and out, then, as the
vagina got bigger, two, then 3 fingers; at the same time
alternately kissing the femmes mouth or sucking her nipple.
The love partner moans, arms wrapped around her lovers
body, arching her back, the butch slides down the femmes
raptured body, and goes down, again sucking her clitorus,
while her fingers move in and out of her vagina at the same
time. The Fem climaxes moaning, her body hot, shuddering
in short jerks, a sob deep in her throat.

Now the butch stands over her mate at the side of the
bed. The femme caresses the masculine womans thighs.
Carefully she moves back the skin of her labia with her
fingers and tenitively flicks the tip of her tongue, exploring,
tasting, seeking the clitorus. She cups her hands around
the butches buttocks, pulling the butch to her, till her
fuzzy head is burried in pubic hair & gets the womans
sex in her whole mouth, sucking, & the butches hips thrusting so that her sex goes up & down on the womans lips
in short jerks. But she doesn't come that way, instead,
gently pushes her mate back on the bed, the femme spreads
her legs for her, slowly sliding up around her body, as
she gets between them, the butches pussy against the
femmes & pumps fast 'till the heat building up inside to
a climax, pounding to a finish, a huge explosion like her
whole body sobbing, or breathing. Hearts still beating,
totally relaxed they lie beside each other. Then, they repeat this proceedure for at least one more go round, but
probably two. Three orgasms each, in other ways, maybe
69. The two of them sharing. They are both starved for
a woman, it's been such a long time. The beginning of a
good thing. . .

Now, we exit the butches skull, as she sits, twirling ice

in the glass, eyes staring into space, not a trace of what she's thinking betrayed on her cool face.

So, she was in Soulville, and there she met a woman.

Suzie Q was being a hooker. But not for long. Fast talking, gum smacking, red nail polish. She bes faaasssst!

'I told her I was a player from New York, tho actually I'm from the susnset district 30 blocks away. And that my name was Gamine, and she couldn't pronounce it & called me Gama, like in Gamma ray. All night long & informed me *her* name was Suzie Q. But occasionally she'd slip up and say she was Mildred Johnson. For instance, "My mother told me, Mildred, you. ." And ect. With all these lies we told from the get go, we were destined to go far. Even if for no better reason then to see what it bes like.

Now I only told her I was a player because I know a ho when I sees one. Actually I'm a draftsperson. I draw blueprints for an Archetect firm. I'm a square. I just told her I was a player, I thought it would make her feel more at home. I didn't want to brag up my good fortune or tell her what I have because her life wasn't going well, I could see that. Black & blue marks over her pretty skin. Her life was on the rocks, & so she was being snotty.

Her name was 'Suzie Q. 21 years old.' But probably younger. She had a man—Flash Gorden named after the cartoon hero—his street name, and she was contemplating leaving him. Tired of his mandhandling her. I thinks to myself, 'Oh oh, trouble.' And also, 'Why can't the black sistah keep her shit together? Why they always have to complicate thangs by having a no good nigger—of either sex—in the background?'

However, against my better judgement, I gave her my phone number—the real one, at the apartment I was staying at. I guess she made me curious.

4.

Later in the week one night as the New York Player was squeezing into sleep over the threshold, RANG RANG! Goes the phone.

It was Suzie Q.

Her soft voice greeted the butch from the other end of the line, as that brown body uncurled amidst a sea of powder blue sheets. "May I speek to Gamma Ray please?"
"GAMMA RAY ? WHAT ? WHO ? HUH ?" The butch says. For a minute this went on. She practically had to fight with the misterious caller telling her there was no Gamma Ray there, until she recognized the voice. Suddenly the rememberance of that alias she'd given flooded back into mind, & the whole evening came back. The vision of a pretty woman in a pink outfit. "OH. *OHH* ! DIS IS ME !" The butch said at last, wiping some sleep out of her brain. "Uh, sorry. . I thought you was someone else."

"*WHO* ? Your old lady ?" She queeried.

"Naw. I ain't got an old lady." The stud says sleepily— and that was mistake number two.

At the other end of the line in a ramsacked motel room, Suzie Q sat on the edge of the sofa. Thick lips had just a faint hue of lipstick—the rest worn off. Her eyes wide, glazed. A combination of no sleep alcohol & pills. The young woman spoke into the phone: "It's Flash Gordon he's driving me crazy. He just gave me an ass whuppen. My haid hurts. And he told me 'BITCH BLIP DE BLOP DE BLOOP DE BLAM !' So I tried to kill myself. I took 20 black beautys and I been up since Monday." (It was Friday.) "So I thought I'd call you." And, without even a, 'let me tell you what happpened can you spare a few minutes ?' she launches into a detail blow by blow description of the unconscious workings of her life.

In a monotone voice, yet gabbing a mile a minute, Suzie went on. It seems she had been down on the strip—those few blocks of motels, and delapelated buildings known as the red light district, in Pappys, one of the drinking & feeding joints where the hustlers hang out, and, as usual, she was acting crazy. Pappys needs a paint job, has an uneven flo', 10 stools with ripped vinel covers. They sell chicken, soda pop & the ladies of the evening go in there to get out of the cold & off their feet. Also, much dope exchanges hands.

"This old man shuffles up to me gurl, he's got a face like a bulldog, and snaggle toothed 'n he's so black yuh could paint a white line up his back and use him for a street, 'n he growls, 'how about some pussy on credit ? I'll pay you Friday, I gets my social security.' 'NOT IN LIFE !' I says. And turns on my heel to end the conversation.

"But the old farmer taps me on the sholder; 'Well then,' he says, 'What about $10. It's all Ah got.' I replied; 'I ain't fucken' fo' free, it's $20.' He says, 'I'll give you $10 and some weed.' 'Cash only.' I replied cooly.

" 'I'll get the $20.' He says. 'Will you be here in half an hour ? I got a buddy who owns the gas station down the way, I can get it from him sugar.' Now I knows about this old man, he likes to slobber all over you, 'n there's no way I'm gonna date him, not with all those other tricks riding around. He's nasty. It's not worth the trouble.

" 'Naw, not today.' I says. 'I ain't doin no fucken' tonight, I'm tired.—My feet hurt.' 'But,' he says, 'Ah just want to. .' And I walk away. See I just don't want to be bothered with no tricks.Period. And I'm determined to have a party with no tricks. Period. No-body slobbering on me, grabbing on me, trying to run their sorry game down on me or nothing. Period. And I'm determined to have a party time and treat *me* right tonight. I'm feeling independant, and gonna do what I wants to do.

"So I walk over to the jukebox, but the old man shuffles after me and says, 'Well honey, all I want to do is eat you out.' By this time I'm sick of him girl, he's so *urgly*, so I says, 'NOT UNLESS YOU CAN FIND A RUBBER TO FIT YOUR FACE.' And EVERYBODY all up and down Pappys howels with laughter.

"So that took care of that. I looks at the rows of bad soul hits on the jukebox lit by blue & orange lights & wishes I had a dime to play. If I dated the old man I'd still have that time to account for to my man & so I couldn't spend the money anyway, so what's the difference? Now I was drunk and highsiding. It ain't nothing but a party.

"The heat's outside, checking ID's so rows of hookers are lounging around, they can't work. No pimps nowhere. Just chit-chatting, shooting that bullshit—talking about their mens, bragging up their mens dicks, they mens clothes, they mens rides, they mens this and thats, how good they mens treats them, while underneeth everybody in the place knows they niggers ain't worth shit.

"So the walls of Pappys are ringing with cuswords and loudtalk & all the hos getting bold with no mens around to keep them in line. Frankly it looks just like the gay bar. All womens. I'm thinking on this in secret. I'd never admit this to none of them bitches down at Pappys, they's never let me hear the end of it."

The clock on the wrist of a hooker flashes red numerals an instent then goes out. She tosses her hand impatiently. Time ticks. Suzie Que is down the bar gabbing just as loud as the next gal.

Meanwhile, RANG RANG ! Goes the phone inside a tiny motel room. A hefty man lies on the couch watching TV in a fur lined hat, bare chest, fur trimmed trousers with suspenders & bare feet. Toenails polished —clear. Pimp style. He rolls off the couch, grunts, runs his hand over his thick jaw, there is stubble on it. He has thick black eyebrows. Walks across the floor, and grabs the ringing phone in his huge meat-chopping hand.

Down at Pappys, Suzie gabs on into the night with any ho who will listen. The heat is gone, the girls are back outside at work—but she's feeling independant, and not in the mood. She don't know it, but the grapevine is simmering. A nosey bitch has snitched to her man, and her man calls Suzies man and runs down the story:

"What's wrong there at the crib Flaaasssh my man ? Is you getten weak, you can't manage yo' ladies no mo' ?" Came an ignorant drawl, snake-like thru the phone, hostilly. "Word has it yo' bitch Suzie *Que* turned down a $20 date with a regular trick 'n all she had to do was lay up there with her legs cocked and let the freak suck her off, man. One of my bitches dated him last week."

5.

3 am on the ho stroll. Black night streaked by silver from the lampposts. WIZZZ of cars passing by outside. Tired ho's is gabbing indoors. The heat is gone, but so is the tricks. And that's when a bitch challanges Suzie Q, coldly dropping the fact that Flash had paid that white woman to go out with him, and at least her man nevah *nevah* did nothing that chicken shit; dropped this like a penny

into an empty collection plate so it rattled in silence—rubbing salt in the wounds.

Suzie Q gave some smart answer, perrying the knife thrust, as cold bovine eyes of the older ho's studied her, however they didn't have long to judge her expression—to see the effect of their words,—time was precious and there was too much other stuff to gab about. Secretly all the whores were eager to say their piece—their piece about something, even if they had to dream up a piece to say, being they didn't have nothing exciting to talk about—except millions of bragged up dollers that they would never see again,(that they never had in the first place, but if they had had, they still wouldn't have, because they greedy mens choaked their purses wringing every last cent out and made them turn it loose.)

Ms. Que kept up her front—a nonchalant smile, eyes behind sunglasses wouldn't reveal much anyhow. But her brain was smoking. Now that had been on her mind for weeks. A white bitch Flash had met in a club waitressing. She worked the San Francisco stroll & dealt dope on the side. She meant plenty money, and Flash was trying to get her to choose, but he had blown his cool by buying her more then one drink. The dice shook up in the fickle fist of fate, rolled out—no dice.

He'd blown $100 taking her out—she'd out-hustled him. A bill—flushed down the toilet for all the good it had done them. Now, this had been working in the back of Suzie Que's mind for weeks. How she'd worked tooth & nail for that hundred, hustling her ass up and down Grove street. At least Flash could have got him an outfit, or put the down payment on a ruby ring to show for it.—But what did they have? Hard feelings.

"The more I thought about it, the madder I got.

"4 am rolled around & I didn't have the first penny to break luck of that evening. —And I'd been out since 9 pm. Well, I was mad as a muthafucker. Mad about not having my kids. Mad about not having no money. Mad about that $100 Flash had blown. Mad that I haven't got nowhere since I been in the fast life—but empty praise from my man, and yes he takes care of my clothes and the room rent, but I'm not getting nowhere, and I'm mad, but I'm scairt too. Eight hours at work and nothing to show for myself.—In Flash's book that's enough warrents for a whupping. And I didn't have change for a dime girl. Not even to call one of my regulars. A trick who'se always good for $30.

"I was mad, so I went in the toilet of Pappys and wrote with my lipstick on the walls:
'FLASH GORDEN AIN'T SHIT, THE NIGGER SPENDS HIS LADIES $ ON SQUARE BITCHES. ASK ANYONE. ONE OF THE BEST NIGGERS TODAY IS BILLY THE KID.'

"Then I pulled down my panty hose hiked up my skirt and pissed into the toilet.

"Now I knew Billy the Kid my man couldn't *stand*. The nigger was lame. Wore a pee-yellow hat, piss pants & a yellow suit jacket the color of dried pee, and it was the ultimate insult to use my mans name & this lame tin-head niggers name in the same breath. But I was smoking. And then I lipsticked a big red X thru the notice that said
'FLASH GORDEN GIVES COCK & COKE TO HIS BITCHES.'

"That I'd wrote the week before—to brag him up to the other ladies down on Grove street, tho we all knows ain't none of them niggers no good 'cept Charlie Brown, and he an old nigger and can't take care of but one bitch. And also X'd out

'FLASH GORDON IS A BITCHES DELIGHT, GIVES PLENTY COCK AND COKE & TREATS HIS WOMENS RIGHT.'

"I smoked a joint, and adjusted my wig in the mirror, and reapplied my make up—using a purple tube, being I'd squashed the color I was wearing making signs. When I got out it was 5 am, and the streets was empty. But it was still dark, and it looked like tricking time to me! But no action.—The ho's ain't heard of daylights saving time I guess."

Suzie Que walked wide-legged down the street in her too-big shoes grumbling to herself & trying to think up an excuse to tell Flash when she got home & didn't have no money to show. Down past the stoplight in the middle of the Boulevard some fucked-up whore was challanging the world with sex. A sorry creature in a maxi coat, red, with a red hood, down to her ankles, short skirt, hard painted face. She had reached the border line between her profession—and psycosis. And this was apparent. Slowly she sauntered in front of a lane of traffic. The car slowed to a stop and the whore strutted across its path terribly slowly, staring at the occupants of the car in a manner, suggestive.

"DO YOU WANT A DATE ?" Sex power welled up in her body. It was sad. The totality of her being focused into this one act—screwing for money. The complex human organism reduced to one function. Her face was stone. Painted many colors, and many fools had worshiped her. Now she was getting ugly, her heart was a hidious mess. She might spend 16 hours on the street and only come back with $5.—Which she sparechanged. Her manner was frightening. She was insane.

The little trooper in the pink dress strode along, pointed

toe shoes first, thick mouthed with a wad of gum. Her eyes in the gutter contemplating. Where oily water was green with streeks of silver.

"And I think about Janice. She's not payen' the police & the reason her not payen' the police 'cause she's got something on the judge. Because he the one bought some pussy. She know the whore-detective too, for the simple reason he's getten' some leg. I think about Janice & I gets mad. See, Janice a call girl, and she don't give up no money. She's her own selfs private call girl. I know this broad don't have no pimps or *nothing*. And I don't care *what* my man tell me about how all self-respecting call girls *he* know has a nigger they gives their money too, I knows for a fact all call girls don't give up their $."

Suzie walked on, grumbling. The motel lights were on, and a few cars drove down the boulevard. Her shadow was 15 feet high diagonaly on the pavement cast from an angle of the neon lights.

She ambled past the "YO' MAMMY IS A HO" sign spreypainted in huge red letters. Where as in Berkeley the hippies sprey paint buildings with things like "DOWN WITH THE FACIST PUPPET GOVERNMENT IN VIET NAM !" But on Grove street, 'bout the best they can do is: "YO' MAMMY IS A HO & SO IS YO' PAPPY." And somebody chalked, "YO' PAPPY IS A PUNK," under *that*.

She walks up from Grove street to the main intersection and sashayes into a fancy restaurent. Air-conditioned, rows of booths, roomy, tastefully covered in gold immitation leather, with a view out of plate glass windows. Decor of wrought metal and wood. Several waitresses bustle about, check pads in their hands, in spiffy uniforms. Her heavy lidded eyes appraise the scene—nobody's in there she knows. She sits down at the counter & orders a coffee & stirs 4 teaspoons of sugar in it; takes the metal container in her brown hand with chipped nails, and pours in as much cream as will fit in the cup. And vows to sit there 'till somebody she know comes in—because she don't have a quarter to pay for the coffee.

"I has my 2 twenties, even, hid in my stocking, but I ain't gonna break that, that's to give to my momma for the kids. And so I sit there waiting, and stiring. And waiting, and stiring. And waiting, and stiring. And I think back to how life bes like when I was a square bitch."

6.

Suzie had been working in a Convelescent Hospital, making $90 per week for turning the old folks over in bed, & cleaning up their shit; and changing dirty linnins. Always a tender heart beneeth her fast exterior, the sight of the helpless old patients had always wrung her guts, but they made her mad too.

They couldn't control their bowels & pissed & shit over everything. They needed help. Often laying in their own excreetment for hours until an aid could tend to them. There was work to be done. It had been a depressing job, one that left her drained not only physically, but emotional-ly—tho she hadn't realized it. It seemed every job she got was like that. She had gave up trying, and become a whore. Bowed down to the god of money. Down on her knees before the negitive god of material possessions. But whoring left her mind drained too—so she stayed high on pills or Marajuanna.

"While I worked at the Hospital I lived in the 24th street Projects. Had a nice little apartment only $160 a month.

119

One bedroom for my kids, & one for me. I had my furnature, stereo, records—buying on time—and, tripple locks on my front door.

"I was getting foodstamps and just making it. Medical paid the doctor. And I took my kids around the cornor for my mother to keep while I worked.

"This is the story. This is the T. The Truth. Three dykes who were hypes lived across the corridor, they on welfare, two of them, and another one who don't live in the building, but always over there partying. You can see their apartment across from mines down the balcony. Now, everybody in these projects is working folks. It's not really projects, a landlord—a white man owns it, but it might as well be, everybody so poor they getting some kind of aid. Nigger downstairs work in a gas station. Lady across the way is a nurse, she got four kids. Sistah upstairs had two kids school age, and while they in school she was enrolled in college herself. One lady a Nurses Aid. In other words, all the folks in the building was hard working but these three hypes who was home night & day and had the building to themselves & played music & stayed loaded.

"So of course they knew when folks was going to be home and not.

"One evening I gets home from work, I see my three locks ripped off the front door.—They was still locked, but the wood pannel on the door frame was ripped out, & the locks hanging. My heart lept into my throat. I goes inside. The place is a mess. First thing I see is one of my big ole lamps broke, smack dab in the middle of the flo'. The 2nd thing I see, my stereo gone. I turn around. My clock radio gone. My wall clock—a sunburst with gold plated reys 4 feet long—gone. Lamps, big red table lamps made of red glass, one gone, the other busted. TV gone, luckly I still hadn't got my color tv, but my black & white, gone. Silverware, dishes, pots & pans still in a pile in a sheet in the middle of the kitchen, they'd been fixen to take too, but somebody in the building must have come home. They took everything they could carry. I had locked my closet door girl, had a combination padlock on that, so they didn't get my clothes or my jewlery. I have $400 worth of jewlery. I'm pissed. Plus, now they know what *else* I have.

"First down on the couch and cried. Then I calls the police. I go out and unlock the three locks and bring 'em inside. I call the landlord & tell him he's got to come by and put some new wood in the doorframe. I can't go out of my house because there's no way to lock my door.

"I draw a chair up in front of the door, and cry myself to sleep. Sleeping on my 6 foot long leather couch. It's my pride and joy.

"The landlord finally fixes the door, but I wait 2 days and miss 2 days work & loose 2 days pay.

"So, one night, I'm just starting to get things together, the kids have been staying over to my mothers, I'm sitting on my 6 foot long leather couch, house quiet, you can hear a pin drop. No music, no radio, no TV.

"Here come a tap on my door. I look out, there, like death hanging in my doorway one of them mangy-looking hypes from across the way. She looks like syphillis has eaten her to the bone. Her name is Buddy. The one that don't even live in the building girl, and she give me some lame excuse—in a funny sounding voice, ask me, 'Oh, was my kids home?' And all this stuff. And I says 'No, my kids at my mothers.' And I knew they were fixing to rob me.

"I had to go to work the next night. Everything's cool when I get home. I breath a sigh of relief.

"The following week I goes to work on the night shift. I

come home that morning, the couch is gone. The three door locks is busted off.—Still locked.

"I sat down on the floor with my paycheck in my hands and cried & cried.

"All week the three dykes acting all homey, up in my face grinning, 'Oh how are you today Suzie ? Oh that's fine.' & knowing I know it was them what robbed me, and all I want to do is get out of that building girl, just move away. It's so depressing. I tell the police, they say theres little they can do, but they take down the information.

"Now, ten days later the lady down the hall what's in college, & me bumps into each other and she invites me to a party. It's across the way and down on the first floor, at the Nurses house. I figure it'll liven me up, I'll have a few dranks, smoke some Marajuanna. I walk in girl, and there's my couch sitting there. Six feet long, just as pretty as you please, against the wall right as you come in, like a centerpiece, so you can't miss it. My leather couch. The dikes had sold it to my neighbor. Ain't that cold ? And the bitch had bought it. Now nobody twisted her arm and made her buy that couch— what a slap in the face.

"Here I am invited to a party & sitting on my own couch—in somebody elses house.

"I don't think the Nurse knew it was mines, but I'm sure somebody had told her by now.

"So I talk to the police, I gets my couch back. Now the Nurse ain't speeken to me, and the three hypes don't know nothin. I just give up. My furniture gone. Lamps gone, and me still paying on it $25 per month, and not making but $92.50 a week & broke. Can't even afford to keep my kids, & giving all my foodstamps to my mother to take care of them. Plus, everytime I pass by Pappys on the way to the busstop the girls talking shit about how good it is in the fast life, how they make $90 a night, and more, and my

$90 a week is chump change to them, plus they pays no income tax.

"So, I gets a job dancing, nights. Switch my shift to days at the Convelescent Hospital. In a bar, shakeing my ass. I'm determined to get as much money together as I can, fast, pay off my debts—on the stuff that's been stolen & I don't even have no mo', and get me a bankroll and start all over again. To climb out of this hole if it kills me. Scheduled myself to work 16 hours a day, 2 jobs. Come home & sleep on the bare flo' every night. I'm gonna save money in the bank, and then move into a building that's got security and a lobby with bells you got to press to let anybody in,—and get insurance.

"I work two weeks. Making $300 at the Go Go club, that's including tips. Then I starts to get spoiled. I quit the Convelescent Hospital. Just didn't go in one day and never came back. I'm sick of working & not getten' no where. I know I can play my tips up to $200 a week if I'm nicer to the customers, & not so fiesty.

"By this time I'd turned 20, and it wasn't hard to pass myself off as 22.

"The Mafeosa owns it.

"They crooked & don't care if the girl lies about her age, but they cheep too, and expect you to work for your money. There's a stage built right up on the bar. You have to get up in these old mens faces & take off your clothes. They pay $3 admission, and $3 for a drink. And they have to keep drinking so the Mafia can keep charging. Durring the break the girls got to go out and sit & talk to the mens in the audience—'cause the men got to buy us a drink for talking to them. We get paid 25 cents on each $3 drink they buy us. The bartender just gives us colored water, or orange juice, 'cause we have to drink most of it, and otherwise we'd get drunk.

"Well one night the girl ahead of me, she has an act she does it on a love seat. The love seat swings down from the ceiling. Well, this night, the love seat got stuck half way down, and the girls tuggen' on the love seat grunting & cussing & has missed the beat and is messing up her act. The love seat has 4 tassles on it, and she's tugging on the tassles and one breaks off & she fell on her ass, her big behind goes flying thru air; and the men tipped her like nothing crazy. So, I figured I'd fall on *my* ass 'cause I wanted that money too, you understand.

"So that was the night Flash Gordon was in the audience. Pimps hang out in the go go joints, always got their hawk-eye out for some woman who ain't choose a man to work for yet. Well, this night I had it planned, how I was going to fall down, and whoop & holler & carry on, and girl I came out, kicking my heels, step, step on time, and kick once, and kick twice and then KICK! And MISS!—Like I re-hersed, but fell off the bar and broke my toe. Now I hadn't planned on doing that; I got tips! $20 in tips just for that one show, but next morning my toe had turned blue & I went to the hospital and the doctor put my whole foot in a cast.

"I couldn't work. Flash Gordon had gave me his phone-number & I had gave him mines. He came by to see me. I was broke, my leg in a cast & couldn't dance. Flash sat there on my leather couch in his green suade jumpsuit with silver studs down the sides, and a green widebrimmed hat, and a furcoat over his arm and rings on each finger. He went in his pocket and peeled off some bills and handed it to me. To pay my rent. It was so kind of him girl, I was so gratefull and in a jam.

"So, that's how I met my man. He rescued me. I went to work for him soon as I came out the cast about 2 weeks later.

"I was so gratefull I wanted to pay him back, but pussy didn't move him none. He was a man gambling for bigger stakes. I couldn't reward him with *me*, so it had to be something else he liked. I listened. He explained how he had a proposition in which we could both benefit & be equal partners. There was a lot of money envolved. My ears perked up!

7.

"Well pay Mr. Gordon back I did, and then some.

"So here I'm sitting up in the restaurant and it's 6:30 am. And I'm deciding the fast life is not for me. I've been in it 4 months & should have paid enough dues, but I'm not getting no where in the fast life either. At least when I was working I had my little place with my kids, my furnuture, my records and my head on my sholders. I think I've lost my head. At least I had $90 a week that I could see—befo' I paid the bills, plus I came and went when I please and *nobody*, my momma, my kids, some nigger, or the police, NOBODY was telling Suzie Que what to Do! Yuh Dig!

"And now I don't have nothin. And Flash steady reminding me how much he's done for me, 'BABY AH HEPED YUH WHEN YUH DIDN'T HAVE NOWHERE TUH TURN—WORKING FOR THE MAFIA, WOULDN'T NOBODY HEP YUH BUT ME.' But I'm adding up the score, of how much I've brung him and it don't quite figure out. 'BABY, IT'S A BUSINESS PARTNERSHIP, WE GOING PLACES TOGETHER.' Is his refrain, but that's always tomorrow, & I ain't been no place yet, but standing out on the cornor of Grove street trying to duck if I see some body who knows my momma drive by."

The gold decore of the restaurant was brightening as the sun rose in the east, beaming thru the plate glass windows, and scouraging the ghost of artifical light into a shadow. The rows of booths were empty, sat one after another down the long room. The brilliant sun rose in the sky. One waitress was on duty. She had only a few customers scattered around the counter.

Suzie Q is thinking. Her false eyelashes blink, her mouth in a pout. One chipped fingernail of one finger taps her lip. All of a sudden, determination came over her. Gets up, and walks out—without paying. It's been 4 hours & it's a different waitress on the new shift.

Grey morning. The bedraggled Peacock, Suzie Q. walks listlissly off the scene.

"By then the dream of independance was fading girl. My feet hurt so bad & I was broke. So I went home. I was too tired to be scared. Have yuh ever felt that way? Too dog tired to even be scared? I'd been out all night, half the morning and didn't have a cent to show. And I wasn't going to touch my kids money in my stocking. That I had promised the Good Creator not to do, or may lightening strike me dead!

"I gets back to the motel, & Flash Gordon is seeing double. He's standing there bigger-then-life in his suspenders studded with rhinestones. Fur hat on his head—adding an additional ten inches onto his height of 6'5" bringing him to over 7 and a half feet tall; alligator shoes with fur tassles, and his 250 pounds packed into a satin shirt & fur-trimmed trousers, and drenched in O'de cologne from his wiskers to his toes, that I bought him, and rings on each finger.—Each paid for by one of his bitches, who he had blown by acting rank, or who was doing time in the penetentary. Four inch platform shoes esculated his height

again to over 8 feet tall! And me only 5'5"! I stumble
across the threshold, my mouth open prepared to tell a
lie, & Gordon grabs me, yanks me inside slams the door,
rips off my coat, grabs in my stockings & brangs out the
$40.

"It might have saved me from a near-death beating.
'IT'S FOR MY KIDS!' My brain screamed, but I barely
wispered it. Gordon snapped the two twenties between
his beefy brown paws. He wasn't satisfied with this amount
of money I had, and, worse, the story of what
I'd said to the trick down in Pappys had got back to the
crib before I did.

"His face was thunder with jagged lightening instead of
eyebrows: 'WHY DIDN'T YOU ACCEPT THAT $20?
WHERE YOU BEEN FUCKEN AROUND ALL NIGHT?
YOU AIN'T BEEN ON THE STROLL! WHAT YOU BEEN
DOIN' BITCH! OFF SOMEWHERE FREEKING OFF FOR
FREE?' And BAM! Slaps me across my face with one fist.
Now the nigger wouldn't care if I was freeken' off with
King Kong, just as long as it's not for *free*. 'WHERE IS
MY MONEY!' He screams. And POW! Hits me from the
other side with his left hand. The echoes vibrate off the
tiny motel room, & 'fore I know it girl, I'm on the floor,
and Gordon's 'bout to start kicking me, but, he says:
'BITCH, I'M GONNA LET YOU OFF THE HOOK DIS
TIME, BEING THAT YOU BRUNG ME DIS $40. I'M
GONNA GIVE YUH *O N E M O R E C H A N C E*, BUT
IT'S THE LAST, BITCH! YOU GONNA GET BACK OUT
THERE SOON AS IT GETS DAY AND THE TRICKS
RIDING AND YOU GONNA STAY OUT THERE AND
HO!' AND DON'T COME BACK HERE WITH LESS
THEN 200$, THAT'S *MY* MONEY YOU MESSEN WITH,
YOU *OWE* ME THAT $200! I BEEN EXPECTING $200

ALL *NIGHT*! & YOU BRANG ME A MUTHAFUCKING
$40! *BITCH*! YUH AIN'T QUALIFIED BITCH! YUH
LOW DOWN NASTY *HO*'!' And last thing I hear him say
he's giving me till tomorrow, & I got to get back out on
the street when it gets light and he's going to kick my ass,
and he's putting on his coat, his wiskers bobbing up and
down on his jaws from saying 'BITCH BITCH BITCH!' O-
ver and over, and kicks me in the head for good measure
with the toe of his Alegator shoes, and slams out the door.
The day has broke. The record player's going round and
round. And Flash Gordons last kick must have knocked
me out cold, 'cause there I was laying on the flo', and I
had this dream:
   "The lights went dim in the motel room, but a brighter
light took it's place. I heard a rushing sound, like the wind,
or the flapping of a sheet on the washline. I was in heaven
girl. I'm convinced of it. Anyways, it was some place
I've never been befo' in my life! That's the only way I can
describe it. Heaven. And all of a sudden, there was the most
tremendous feeling of peace came over me. And happiness,
just like an ocean running in, covering me up."
   Suzie was nearing the end of her tale. The foggy voice
at the other end of 'Gamine' who sat, in pajamas at the
edge of her bed, wiggling her brown toes & clearing her
throat for the upteenth time.
   ".. I was... how do you say it.. I was everywhere,
I could feel everything.. my body was different... Do
yuh understand? I could feel things & see things, like I
was watching from a great distance.. and I could feel my
life and the mistakes I'd made.."
   "My God", Gamine is thinking as she passes a brown
hand with square tipped fingers over her face, stifeling a
yawn for the umpteenth time this last 30 minutes, "this

woman's crazy. She's popped them pills & gone stark raving boocoops mad." "YEAH YEAH." She spoke into the phone, feigning enthusiasm. So Suzie Q. rattled on.

"So there came a voice, not a voice I heard with my ears, but I *felt* the voice all thru me—it was like waves, or warm waves of water, but it wasn't water. Just waves. . & I felt such a love inside of me. . . it's never happened before in life, that's all I can say. ." She snapped, a little uncertain.

"Yeah." Says Gamine.

"So, this *Being*, God, or whoever asks me to make an account of myself. What I had done, what I was proud of doing, and the bad things too. The Being was full of light and very kind. I knew there was no anger at me for anything I'd done. The Being didn't say this, I just knew that's what was happening. . and that's why I was there."

So Suzie Que had began to go back over her life. In flash-backs that rolled into vision like the waves of a crystal lake parting, a knowledge imparted to her, closing, then a new rememberance. The knowledge, the—higher wisdom present, indicated how things could have been, instead of how they were. At age 2 if there had been kindness shown to her instead of selfishness. Or age 15, if there had been understanding, instead of neglect. In a matter of moments they traced the slow deformities of our human existance.

The universe is waiting, around us, and the absolute veil had been lifted from her eyes & for an instant she saw the truth.

In the dim motel room, Suzie groped for the words. "I can't explain it girl. The Being, it must have been Jesus, or God—it was much more advanced. And pure. And the Being wanted to know where I was going wrong in my life.

"And we watched together as scenes unfolded—it was the strangest dream I've *evah* had—that's why I don't think it was a dream. We saw everything.

"Afterwords a sort of feeling vibed thru me; the voice finally said: 'Suzie Que, you were guilty of getting pleasure out of pain. . . . . *And* of stiring up the shit.'

"I bowed my head. It was true. The Being knew me better then I did. But I also could confess my entire self, because I knew the Being wasn't a judge, wasn't banging down no gravel, stony faced in a black robe behind the bench. The Being was so *infinate*. It was *kind*. Girl, I knew if I'd stayed up in heaven one minute longer I wouldn't have wanted to come back.—But I did. I had to, for my kids sake. The Being told me that.

"It was all fading, but I was still trying to talk to the Being.—Without words kind of talk, like my mouth was just. . a puppet, made out of rubber, but my *feelings* were talking—a lot better then I could have! 'Well. . .' I told the Being, 'I worshiped Gods who looked just like me!' And the Being understood. It knew, and I knew I was right, but I *never* could have thought of something like that in my normal state. And what my thoughts meant was— *niggers*. That I worshipped niggers. Niggers with fingers dripping full of rings, and platform shoes, and satin capes and bes snorting that coke and shit. I thought they was the finest thing walks Gods green earth.

"Then the scene was starting to fade; I held onto it as long as I could, I was still asking, but I couldn't hear my voice no mo'. I was hungry to hear more information.

"Then the Being said something I forget, then, '. . . . . because you'd rather accept death every day—in ordinary ways.' And again it was so wise & tender, I knew the Being was completely on my side. And I also was given the knowledge of what was meant. I pictured them whuppings folks have gave me, & the police messing with me... a million little... everyday things like.. dying, only I hadn't seen it was death at all.

"The Being didn't say nothing more, but flashed me a vibe of love. And once more I felt its voice add, '.... instead of taking one giant step.' And then I *knew* part of me had to die. The dead part had to go, I mean, a lot of my old ways.

"And I was emersed in an alluminating light—from God. There had been a lot more words. A lot more knowlcdge given to me, but I was beginning to forget it already. But one change I could see it all meant, simply I was going to straighten my life out when I returned. Get off the fast track. I was almost *eager* to get my job back at the Convelescent Hospital. I couldn't *wait* to—while I was in heaven. It seemed like a very outstanding thing to do. To help those old people, & to love my kids. To give them all the love I had. I was full of a tremendous energy to do these things. And I could barely talk, but I heard myself manage to say, 'I'LL DO IT!' Like I was telling the Being goodby.

"And then I woke up."

There was a pause on the line. Gamine cleared her throat.

"So," says the voice over the phone from the motel room, somewhat quieted, very serious; "so I was sent back down here, & here I am!"

"God gave you another chance." Gamine says, glumly.

"Yeah, somethin' like that."

"Huh."

"Only now I don't feel as strong. *Then*, I couldn't do wrong. I was full of energy. I knew exactly what to do, and couldn't wait to do it. I wasn't one bit tired.. but now. . . . *WHEW*." She says.

"I know what you mean."

"And so I wake up." Suzie finished. "And here I was—in life. Totally. I got up off the flo', the stereo's playing the same record, & I looked thru the room, in the bathroom, no Flash Gordon. In the closet, no Flash Gordon. In the foldaway bed, not there. Flash Gordons gone, and now he's gonna kick my ass fo' real!" She says.

**

I'm beginning to feel a vague suspicion. 'Uh oh.' I thinks to myself. I hear the nervousness in Suzie Que's tone, then, she confirms it.

"I'm in a jam honey. . . my bags are packed. . . . Can I come stay with you for a while?" Comes her plantative voice over the line. "Just long enough, 'till I gets back on my feet. . . ."

So my mind is reeling. I've just woke up, I don't even know the womans name. . also I'm impressed. What a bold bitch! She's been to the Hereafter & told God how she's let niggers bes the cause of her misfortune, and appologized & knows she wants to change, and now she was getting one more chance. One more chance. One more chance.—It sounds like a broken record don't it ?

And I'm still mumbling, half asleep, my hair all knotted up on my head when, 45 minutes later, faster then sin she arrives at my front doorstep. She must have got some trick to drop her off. But that ain't nuthin I guess, after all, she got to heaven didn't she ?

Glass

Judy Grahn

She wouldnt eat at the same table with me, that's even what she said. She said it was an old European custom to refuse to sit at table with someone. She meant *if they were lower than you*. So all week, even if she had cooked the meal, she would disappear as soon as the table was set, to her own room---or that was my guess; although maybe she was really locking herself into the bathroom and picking at her nails. They were long enough. Her hair and nails were long, her skirts were short, not that I was interested in that part. I have always liked physical women, who use their bodies in all kinds of ways. Hers was strictly for display.

And not that it didnt bother me, her supposed fragility, her airs and graces. She wasnt easy going, no, not a bit like Ruth; I couldnt believe they were sisters. I always felt like rolling down my sleeves in her presence as if my own arm muscles were an affront, my elbows offensive to her. I always felt like lowering my eyes in her presence, a bad sign, though I never did; that is to say, I tried not to. She seemed flimsy but she was not. She was cruel, even in her own house.

Yet she used me, got me to carry things up and down stairs and in and out of doors for her. One evening I went into her room because she complained so loudly that her window frame was broken, snow was blowing in because it wouldnt close. She would have to call the carpenters, the landlord, the mister-fix-it down the block, and here it was, night already. I tapped the top of the stuck window with my fist and the frame dropped into place, she was amazed. She hadnt thought of that. Or had she? I couldnt tell. I was angry; a woman twice my size. She tricked me. She wanted a practical life but she wanted to buy it--or steal it--from someone else. I wanted to shake her, but she was too tall, and brittle. She would have broken willingly and cut me like a crystal glass. I hated her, even though I was proud that the window was fixed, so easy. A woman like this would never tolerate snow blowing into her bedroom, she would sleep in the hall first, with my blanket, and apologies.

From her room we went downstairs and drank, our first social intercourse, since she was never at the dinner table. My drinking is like drinking; her drinking is like good manners.

Yet I was the guest in this case--not her guest, the guest of her sister Ruth--for two precious weeks, half-gone, and how I wished she would come home from work, NOW.

Here I was in a living room with a woman who paid close attention to the details of good manners, cloth napkins, fixing the meals graciously, setting a meticulous table, commenting to me continually the fine points of her stupid recipes--and then disappearing into her room because she could not bear to eat with me.

I could not understand it.

Now at least she drank with me, or anyhow sipped at her wine, perhaps to thank me for the window? I felt like a clumsy guzzler; and her neat living room settled down on my shoulders like an oblong hump; I hunched over the bottle.

"Do you like the Van Sobret?" she asked, or something like that, which I thought was a musician until I saw she meant the wine and nodded eagerly, too eagerly, while a certain sullenness began to lump in my stomach.

Her glass animals flashed in my eyes. They stood sexlessly around the room, even on the piano no one played. She crossed her legs many times. We had already wound each other up and even the clock tick couldnt make us more nervous. Snow fell outside with an unsatisfactory lack of sound.

"I think I'll go for a walk in the snow," I said, and for a moment she seemed interested; I said it twice more in the course of her sudden stream of chatter, which was all about the people where she worked, as a research analyst or historical assistant or something. I couldnt follow any of it, only her laughing in a high way, her limpid hand orchestrating the upper ranges of her voice. Lilting, they called it. To myself I sounded like a monotonous bass fiddle, and the wine only made me louder and more resinous. I seemed to say nothing but 'yeah'. How had I ever imagined that I was an intelligent, real, full grown person?

"Frances," she lilted suddenly, in my direction, "you're such an adventuress--Ruth should have warned me. You'd never catch me out there--it's practically a blizzard." She glanced at her stockings, her polished cardboard shoes. She laughed, she sipped, her rings flashed. I saw my face reflected in her glasses. I wondered what I possibly could have done, to so offend her.

My face longed for the sting of ice but the wine had turned me to wood. I knew she would think me a fool, clonking downstairs in my good boots and leaving puddles of water on her floor when I returned, like a puppy.

Maybe I should set the table, I thought. Then she would disappear.

I walked around in her living room, coarsely. "You are so restless," she said.

"No. My legs are cramped."

"I brought this crystal back from Vienna," she said, and paused. My only association with Vienna was Vienna sausage, but she didnt pause long enough for me to come in with that line. "It's so beautiful there this time of year." She sighed. She crossed her legs. She was telling me she's travelled. 'Her wine glass was so thin it looked as though it would cut her mouth spontaneously. I imagined patching her up, running over with a washcloth to press to her lip.

Instead I looked out the window where the snow piled rapidly in the trees and icicles reflected the street lamps. It's beautiful *here* this time of year, I thought, and what is travelling except taking a walk around the block with someone you dont know very well. I remembered all the people I had ever eaten with. I saw suddenly that I was Ruth's adventure, her way of travelling. It didnt bother me, to see this. I know very well what women use each other for. This one had no use for me at all. Except to carry her stuff. My mouth felt like it was full of pudding, but I tried again. "Why dont we go for a walk in the snow."

"Oh, no *thank* you," she said firmly. Her foot bobbed up and down at the end of one crossed leg, and she smoothed her tiny skirt--she was a huge woman, a foot and a half taller than me, but she had no pockets so her hands were always all over the place filling up the air in front of her, all around her hair, her face, her clothes. As though constantly checking to be certain everything was there.

"I'm afraid I lead a very mundane life, very slow--and ordinary." She showed me the back of her hand as she made a stiff half-yawn behind it. She had been doing that all night; an abbreviated message.

I cracked my knuckles in a message of my own, and pretended to look out at the sky; no use for her to know how anxious I was for Ruth to come back, though I didnt want to be so drunk when that happened.

Actually I wanted the goddamned woman to leave the room, to at least let me be alone in the living room so I could drink myself into a better frame of mind. And by now I was feeling rash about it.

Her fingernails were making a slight sound as she ran them lightly over one of her glass animals--I wished to punch her and I wished for her to punch me back, to get off the floor with a bloody nose, glasses crooked, face wild and throwing those animals at me until my face streamed from a thousand cuts. *Then* maybe she would eat with me.

Instead I went to the record player and without asking permission, put on a record of Ruth's, an intense rythmic record--and taking another deep slug of wine I proceeded to dance all to myself with my back to everything, going deep into my head the way you do in the bathtub. When the piece was finished I turned around and she had gone.

I am certain she thought that I had made a pass at her.

A Trip to Chicago

Joyce Maupin

From the window of her new apartment in Brooklyn Heights Pauline could see the spires of Manhattan studded with golden light. She was hidden by the vast anonymous city and Doug would not be able to find her. In fact, he would not be looking for her.

It was past midnight when she went to the window again and saw a man standing on the sidewalk below. A motionless figure half-obscured by darkness, both familiar and menacing. She smiled, rejecting the idea as hysterical. Doug had not followed her. If he did know she was here, he would never stand outside. It was she who waited for hours in front of a lecture hall hoping to see him when he left. Doug would come right up, ring the bell and walk in confidently. Tell her pretending to leave for Chicago was a childish trick.

You don't have to go to another city to get away from me he said that morning as they stood at the gate to her Chicago-bound train, around them the casual turbulence of Grand Central. There is room enough in New York for both of us. Pauline shook her head. She had tried it before.

Everything went smoothly and she was sure it looked convincing. She boarded the train, settling down comfortably with an orange drink, a magazine and a book. His latest novel, inscribed to her with the unctuous sentiments he distributed so generously whenever he was pushing a new book. She leaned forward to wave at him. When she

138

reached the 125th Street station in Harlem, she got off, and took the long subway ride back to Brooklyn Heights.

An evening of unpacking cartons, hanging up clothes, lining cupboard shelves and putting away dishes. Pauline went to bed exhausted. It should be easy to get some sleep. She switched out the light and immediately saw his face. I don't love you, she said. He was laughing again, telling her love was appetite in a sentimental disguise. If you want to marry and live in the suburbs I'm sure you can make it. Go to church or go bowling. Meet a wholesome young man.

As he said it his eyes held a different message, drawing her toward him, binding her to his own destructive vision. He had small black eyes imbedded in pasty skin. Malignant eyes that seized on you while the face itself remained impassive. The hard face contradicted by the gentle, cunning hand which caressed her and released a catalyst, illuminating her senses and extinguishing her mind.

She turned in bed, longing for Doug, stretching out her arm for the telephone. The table was empty. There was no phone because she did not want one. That would make it too easy for him to reach her, or for her to reach him. Smiling, pleased that the ruse had worked, she drifted into sleep.

Later the dream roused her and she woke up in a cold sweat, her body rigid. Not a dream but a nightmare. Did she scream out loud? If anyone heard her, they would ignore it the way people do in New York. Tell themselves it's a lovers quarrel so they can go back to sleep.

She tried to focus on the details of the dream before they slipped away. The mask. Running away from a figure wearing a mask. Following her until she reached the bog. A turgid, translucent liquid sucking at her feet. The masked figure came closer. To pull her out or push her in?

Shuddering, Pauline got out of bed. She needed a hot shower, a fresh nightgown and a sandwich. Half an hour later, she felt calm enough to shrug it off. It was natural, under the circumstances, to dream about running away. She dug into one of the cartons for a book and went back to bed, reading until she grew drowsy again.

The next morning it seemed so obvious. What bothered her and brought on the nightmare was the flaw in her plan for escape. In spite of her move to Brooklyn Heights, even though she avoided the likely places, an accidental meeting was possible. Not in the subway—Doug always took taxis. Her apartment was only half a block from the subway. Emerging at the other end, she crossed the street to her office. For a while, it might be a good idea to eat lunch in the employee's cafeteria and go right home after work.

Rather. elaborate precautions, since Doug was not pursuing her! Yet if he knew where she was, he could come, just to show how easily he could get her back. It was enough, seeing him once or hearing his voice.

At the office Pauline felt calm, absorbed by petty details. She did not think about the figure below her window. Not until she got home from work. Then, resisting an impulse to look out and see if he was still there, she told herself that it was a busy street. Even if she did see a man it need not be the same man. Forget him and unpack the books. Pile towels and sheets neatly on the bathroom shelves.

Again that night the dream woke her and she lay in bed trembling, clammy with sweat. The heavy liquid rose higher pulling at her knees. This time she heard them, too, tormented voices from the bodies writhing beneath. The masked figure stood close by. It had to be Doug. He wasn't going to rescue her and he would not shove her in. As I go under, she thought, choking, strangling, screaming for help, he will stand there watching me.

Why didn't she reach out and take off the mask? Why had she run in the same direction as last night, toward the bog?

Now it was more difficult to expel the nightmare and go back to sleep. She sensed an illogical connection between her dream and the figure standing outside. *If* anyone was there. She raised her eyes to stare at the drawn shade. One thing was certain, it could not be Doug. He hated open space, and even on a city street he felt uneasy, hurrying from one building to another, the next speaking engagement or the next woman. He did not care which as long as he got inside and closed the door.

She wondered, would he help me if I got sick? If I lay here dying? He never had enough time. No time to waste.

He had broken a date with her because another woman dropped in to see him. Why go out of your way to see a girl when you have a woman right there? He smiled in answer to her complaint. Monogamy was unnatural. Repressive. He said it with such conviction she almost apologized for trying to repress him.

If you want a man to share your fantasy of true love, keep away from me. He was speaking and at the same time touching her. Again the harsh jubilation overwhelmed her and ebbed away, leaving self-contempt instead of tenderness.

Peggy Morrison had turned on the gas. He drove her to it, they said, but it wasn't true. A normal woman does not kill herself because she loves an unscrupulous man. She can leave him. Pauline had left him many times. It was her fault not his that he got her back by picking up a phone.

While he was really not responsible for the woman's death, his reaction shocked everyone. He did not react at all. He spoke casually with no grief or guilt, not even an excuse. He did not care.

For a long while thoughts and images pressed in, preventing sleep. The next morning she forced herself to get up, eyes swollen and red. Reluctantly she left the security of her apartment for the street. Walking among strangers the threat came closer. But what did the threat consist of—a bad dream, a non-existent man?

In the office, at her desk, she responded to the familiar routine and again felt reassured. It was only on the trip home that she thought about him again, and suddenly found herself believing in him. A man *was* hanging around the apartment building, but why assume he did it to threaten her? He might know the woman upstairs . . . they had quarreled and he wanted to see her again. This evening, Pauline decided, I will check the window every hour. I will make sure.

When she first got home, it was impossible to separate one figure from all the others. So many people were coming back from work, walking along the street. After supper a shadow appeared on the sidewalk. It could be the shadow of a man who was hiding in a passageway between the two buildings.

Pauline tested the bolt on the front door. Closed all the windows and locked them, too. Silly but it helped. I am really afraid, she thought. Afraid to sleep because the dream will come back. Afraid to go to the window again.

She sat up in a chair not sleeping at all, reading and waiting, hoping for the grey sanity of morning. The air grew oppressively close. He was out there although he couldn't be. Did she think he had stepped from her dream to take up a vigil in front of the house? In the morning, if I know he is there, I will be insane.

He was *not* an imaginary man! She decided now that he had nothing to do with Doug or with her dream. There were so many demented men who tracked women through city streets. Every day you read something in the newspaper about a woman getting killed. Had he first noticed her on the day she moved in, started following her?

The next morning she told herself that he could not possibly attack on the half-block between her home and the subway. The streets were too crowded. Hundreds of people hurrying to work. Would he attack at all? Maybe he was following and watching only to arouse her fear.

As soon as she left the house, she felt sure, except that you are never quite sure. You rush to the subway entrance and there are so many people, how can you tell if one of them is moving closer?

Her office seemed safe, possibly because she worked in the center of the building away from windows and outer doors. Here everything functioned mechanically. Machines clicked and hummed on the long rows of desks, precisely lined up. Even the light and air were artificial, produced by other machines. An oasis of safety. She wanted to stay there all night.

That evening she ran from the subway to her apartment building. The elevator was at the top floor so she ran up three flights of stairs to get to her door, drawing the bolt shut with an exclamation of relief.

The air in the apartment stifled her. Suddenly she realized that the place itself was a trap. If anyone broke in, she did not even have a phone to make an emergency call. No one would hear her when she cried out. They never do.

She began sobbing and called him by name. Doug, Doug. If it's you I want you to come in. The sound of her own voice startled her. She was going out of her mind.

Was that the choice? To be with Doug in spite of humiliation and pain, to be with him under any conditions, on any terms, as long as she could see him occasionally? Or madness, a cell with bars at the window where screaming was a part of the routine?

The other woman made a different choice. Turn on the gas and in a little while there will be nothing. Nothing at all. She looked at the stove in her kitchenette. Easy. Except the odor may seep out into the hall and someone may come to your rescue even in New York. Besides it wouldn't do any good. Doug was not going to feel sorry. He was not going to feel guilty. It would not hurt him at all.

She might leave a note that implicated him. No, he would use that, too. Turn it into publicity for his books.

Alive or dead she could find no way to reach him. How do you get at a man who has no feeling? He is impervious, a wall that cannot be breached. Senselessly, your hurl yourself against the wall.

Pauline gasped as she saw the way out. He had physical feelings like anyone else. A knife cutting into his flesh would hurt and the wound would bleed. This time he must react, raising his voice in a cry of pain.

Instead of killing herself, kill him! A murderous joy possessed her. He stood before her and she drove the knife deep, aiming for his heart. He smiled at her thrust and did not bleed. How could she destroy him? She dropped the knife, her hands leaping toward his throat, squeezing it and cutting off breath. The eyes bulged and the tongue protruded but he was still standing there. She had still failed to kill him. In a rage her nails ripped through his flesh. Finally he swayed and fell. She leaned over him. He was monstrous and he was dead. She wanted to spit at the body. No, he was dead, and there was no justification for her hatred. Now she could forget about him.

She sank down on the bed and fell asleep, slept soundly

all night and woke up in the morning feeling refreshed. Last night's fantasy had such force that she almost expected to see his body lying beside the bed.

The air was heavy and stale. She looked around in amazement at the locked windows. It was fortunate that she lived alone. A roommate would have called for an ambulance to take her to Bellevue.

Leaving the house that day was like taking the first step after surgery. Tentative but wonderful because you are on your feet again. Tonight she must celebrate. Call Ruth for dinner and a movie.

She was still afraid. Sooner or later she had to meet him and what would happen to her then? She might turn and run, get as far away as possible, really go to Chicago. Or would his snare close around her, inflaming her body, blotting out thought? Why not ignore him, pass by without speaking at all? It was a question of time. With enough time, she could learn how to handle it.

She saw him on a hundred streets, coming around the corner and walking toward her. Across the way, standing in front of a grocery store. When he came close she knew that it was only a similarity of manner or of build. The passing weeks slowly dulled her anxiety, and she no longer expected him.

Then on an aimless Saturday afternoon she stopped at a Village coffee shop. Reading her newspaper, she was warned by a prickling sensation part expectancy and part fear. She raised her eyes and saw his back. This time she was positive, realizing she had come here because it was one of the obvious places, hoping to find him again and test the strength of her recovery.

The young woman with him faced Pauline and she was arguing, her voice high and excited, hands lifted in apparent protest. With a final angry gesture, she rose and walked off.

Pauline went over to the table. "Doug."

"Hello! Back from Chicago so soon? Didn't you like it there?"

"I never went to Chicago. It was a trick to get away from you. I think it worked." She felt no desire and no hatred. She had been away a long time.

"Christ, you went to all that trouble! It's easy. You just walk off."

"Like the woman who was sitting here with you?"

"Nothing personal in her case. She works for my publisher—my former publisher. I persuaded her to snoop around and find out why they turned down my last book. She just told me it was too much like the others."

He looked tired, eyes puffy and bloodshot, face bloated. He had been drinking heavily for years but he didn't show it so much before.

"You think you got me out of your system?" he asked.

"I think so." She still did not feel the pull, the excitement of seeing him and being close to him again. "I killed you one night. Tore you apart. I didn't know I had such violent feelings."

"Most of us are savage if you get under the surface."

She stared at him remembering the dream. He did not fit. The shape of his head was wrong, the size of his body. He could not be the figure wearing the mask.

A faceless symbol, she thought. That's why I never removed the mask, there was nothing underneath. Then in her mind it was drawn aside and the features began to take shape. With a chill of recognition she saw her own face and realized that she had known it all along, even during those strange days of delirium and fear. Leaving Doug meant that she must learn to live with herself.

The Woman Fables, 1-12

Dell Fitzgerald-Richards

THE WOMAN WOKE

the woman woke with a feeling of heaviness she knew well.
ah that time she thought, another few days . . . at least
i'm not pregnant. though she hardly worried about that
anymore she never seemed to get pregnant mind over matter
she supposed unless it was the years of birth control pills
and the scant blood now. she had never gone to find out
though more male doctors giving her other chemicals never
explaining anything perhaps upsetting a balance that was an
advantage to her.

another month gone by she thought wondering what she
had done in almost 29 days as she lay looking at the sun-
light through the brown and yellow tie-dyed curtains. she
really enjoyed waking up to their coppery colors; she would
never have believed it would have made so much difference
to each day's slow process of waking breakfast school work
and studying. she woke slowly enjoying that misty feeling

of having just woken up and wondered how quickly she could get ready for school thinking it would give her that much more time to lie here. the heaviness was still with her, though it was two days early by her moon calendar.

she couldn't help thinking how strange it was that her body waited for the new moon to bring it release . . . fertility in fullness when the moon was at its height, the cycle begun again in the darkness of the new moon. but she knew the feeling today would not bring her on. no today was still too early she could feel that as she began to dress.

THE BIKER'S LADY WORE A TATTOO

and it didn't matter that the wind snarled her hair or her back sometimes ached. it didn't matter as long as she were riding touching the air feeling the rush of the ground on this mad animal, this motorcycle. his motorcycle. when she leaned back to see the stars at night on some lone country road, they seemed to twinkle just for her. he had paid one-hundred and forty dollars, most of his savings, part of their wedding money on this grumbling beast. but they rode and rode, feeling free as birds.

they rode whenever they were bored, whenever they wanted out. they rode on saturdays, his day off. he rode when he was angry.

it was a lovely honeymoon, the three of them wedded as they were in chrome and steel and flesh, speeding into a make-believe movieland sunset. the vineyards swirled round them, the city lights became a blur in the distance . . . until she tired of riding, of tears blowing down her face and her back aching. she began gardening or had him drop her at a friend's house on saturday afternoons.

he went out alone for a while, as if nothing had happened though it was just him and his cycle, a lonely pair, until sixty was too much for it. gears splattered everywhere, he pushed it down the entrance ramp to escape the speeding cars and leering lights of the monster freeway.

they brought it home in the back of a pick-up truck and it drained oil for another few days, leaving its territorial mark on the concrete walk. when the rains came, they moved it onto the back porch where it sat for the rest of the winter turning into a rusty horse with flat wheels and a frozen horn.

they spoke of the "good old days" and the hundred and forty dollars and watched three o'clock movies on tv for something to do.

SHE READ ZELDA FITZGERALD

with a quarter turn of the kitchen table they created a place to eat where before they had only chopped vegetables. the addition of a green gauze lamp gave coolness and luxuriance to the area. but something about the table insisted on order; she found herself picking up stray newspapers and books, arranging them neatly in piles with edges matching. she even found more boxes to add to the bookshelf in the living room and moved the cook books to the bookcase to make room for the japanese cast iron tea pot, a relic of her first

marriage. it now housed a newly-potted ivy. the old singer
sewing machine she had meticulously polished after removing all extraneous parts held the few remaining books
steadily in place. it was all very just so and she enjoyed
looking at it, knowing she had created it. they had tea at
the table and talked for hours drinking wine in the evening
and being very civilized. they even started cooking though
they never seemed to find the time to actually bake the
eggplant parmesan they talked of that sounded so scrumptuous in the recipe but took so long in the making. they sat
at the table under the pleasant light many an evening
though the straight-back chairs were rickety and not very
comfortable.

she took to reading short stories and stopped studying for
exams. she said her mind functioned better on information
easily digested rather than savoured. reading zelda fitzgerald
for the first time she was surprized at her competence.

though her life had barely changed (they had only moved
the table) there was a perceptible difference. time seemed to
move more quickly. there was less of it. she never got anything done. the edges of her mind felt frayed she began to
nag and feel hemmed in. she could look around and see the
spacious rooms she had tidied where everything was in
perfect order but somehow everything seemed closer the
objects that she had re-arranged seemed as if they would
reach out and touch her pull her over to them to re-arrange
them once more to an even more precise form. the bed she
made every day began to look like an ocean whose waves
lapped over her calling her to it to put a stop to its motion,
to stop its chaos. the curtains wanted opening as soon as
the first ray of sun touched the house. yes they were calling

her. every dish every loose paper and stray towel, every speck of dust cried out to her with a life of its own. ah yes, she had ceased to exist.

THE FISH

she paced the floor once and paced back again as she had done for centuries. a steady walk across the room. in another room the men sat smoking, only slightly different from men eons earlier though once it had been a hall with oaken tables burning candles and the smell of fur. now the cigar smoke only swam under the glare of an electric light and circled the dark green walls. she continued to pace the floor in the other room.

"my mother died many moons ago. why did i come to this?"

he held the highest cards and everyone knew it except his brother who smiled and looked hopeful. he would lose again but he kept hoping lady luck would be on his side one day. the winner looked worried.

"she died alone just like her mother before her. just like i too will die it is only a matter of destroying the body."

he finished the beer slowly, wondering how high his brother would go. he wished she would bring more beer.

she watched the fish as they swam in quick little motions that made them think they were going somewhere. she wondered how long it would take for them to die if brought into the life of her air but she withdrew her hand from the tank without touching them. they only swam past her coming sometimes to look at her though they never said anything.

a few minutes later she faced the electric light with a new feeling. "glad to see you're going to win, honey" she said as she poured the beer over the table and decided to find a new life.

BUY A BROOM

the woman wondered if there were any special significance to the fact that every time she bathed, or even put her hands in water, she caught a cold. she had barely gotten over the last one when this one arrived and it had been going on like this all year. she had tripled the stated dosage of vitamin c and was taking at least one pill of every other vitamin to make sure it worked. she had even stopped watching television for fear the medicine ads were subconsciously making her want to have a cold so she could buy their brand.

she felt very silly associating a cold with getting wet but it was a rather odd coincidence. she had to do something soon; she hadn't had a bath in two weeks.

and right at the back of her mind was this insistent little voice that kept saying "you are turning into a witch, dear, a witch." she had been hearing the voice for several days and instead of going away, it was getting louder. in desperation she finally decided that with the state of transportation being what it was, she'd get a broom and see if she

could fly it. if she could, then she would buy a book of
spells and see what magic she could conjure up to use
instead of washing, washing anything.

HIBERNATION

when the winter came she wrapped her large woolen cloak
tightly around her and told everyone she was flying to rio.
in the morning she would drive herself to the airport alone
and a few weeks later postcards would arrive of the christ
of the mountain the mardi gras the lush vegetation and
unusual birds. in may she would drive up to her house once
again park her car and take up where she had left off six
months or so earlier. she rarely talked about her trips south
and the people of the neighborhood called her the bird
woman behind her back.

what they didn't know was that in fact, she never actually
went anywhere during those long months. they would see
her drive away and they would see a darkened house for the
next months but what they would not see was her return
the very same day in the darkness of the night. what they
did not know was that she was hibernating while an ac-
quaintance she had met on her only visit to brazil would
send postcards to all the designated addresses.

her hibernation was not something she had discovered
accidentally or even in one season. it was something she
had worked up to over a period of years. originally, like
most people, she had withdrawn from the world through
illness. short periods of a week or less a few times a year
that gave her a rest from the daily routine of existence. then

she had realized that it was much simpler (and more pleasant) simply to take to her bed and pretend illness while she ate only the foods she fancied and read books for hours on end. gradually she increased the length of her respite and became less inclined to visitors.

as her period of withdrawal lengthened and regularized itself into a seasonal wintry response she felt she would have to invent a story. hibernation was simply too strange. so remembering her old friend and her pleasant visit one christmas she enlisted her aid and began her formal withdrawal. after a winter or two everything was quite simple. friends and relatives enjoyed their south of the border mail; they even gossiped about her relationship with the friend she visited each half the year.

and while the world continued scurrying around outside she slept ate read watched television and did whatever she wanted in her little house. she was glad to see everyone when she emerged . . . she was so rested she was a totally new person . . . she often wondered if she should tell anyone. it did her so much good she even thought of writing to the president to suggest hibernation as a means of lessening the tension of modern society. but she was too timid. instead she continued her yearly cycle, knowing she had found the secret of existence.

PORPOISES TOO

she had only had the waterbed a week when she started dreaming consistently of water creatures. night after night. each time she would slip off to her dream world to find it inhabited by porpoises dolphins and every imaginable sort of fish (and some she would have never thought existed). she was even beginning to notice green sea plants giant crabs and anemones. it was all very odd.

she would have spoken to someone about it but the way back to daylight was long and quite time consuming. she would wake up in her bed where it was sunny and bright and have only a vague recollection that something strange had happened in the night, only she couldn't remember what. yet each night as she lay down and closed her eyes it would come back to her. even before dozing off she would suddenly recall where she was going and what would happen, as if the daylight hours had never existed. she was afraid and yet she felt a warm glow of familiarity that sent her immediately to sleep.

tonight the way was short and her skin didn't tingle as it first had when she glided into the water. her hands seemed a bit silvery but she thought it must be the moonlight through the water. when she arrived everyone was in a state of anticipation. there were hanging lights and long tables ready for a feast. the dolphins were even more promiscuous and playful than usual. tonight, they said, they were welcoming a new inhabitant.

the next morning when she finally awoke after the long celebration, she thought she had had a dream of a whale lumbering through her bed rocking it like the earthquake that had once washed under her house, lifting it slowly and majestically, like a wave, as it rolled on its way. she remembered a ceremony where everyone had kissed her and she seemed to be standing in the center of a circle. as she rolled over on the beach the sun seemed very bright, oh much too bright. there was sand in her hair and her legs were very stiff but it didn't matter, no . . . she was tired too tired to care. so she rested her arm on the brown seal she was lying next to and drifted back to sleep.

THE HIPPOPOTAMUS

watching the mud move round her day after day flowing smoothly upon her, the hippopotamus swam and floated enjoying the feel of the soft water on her flanks and back. it washed over her in persistent endurance. the spring rains had come early and the water was a liquid velvet flowing around her. only the grey-brown color which so well camouflaged her head differentiated it from the clear waters that swam further on to the sea. but the texture of her dark environment changed rapidly as summer approached. recently the river had begun to slow down: it seemed to be thickening.

though she watched with ever increasing wonder, she made no judgments. she thought that time would stretch on endlessly as it always had done. she noticed the other animals disappearing slowly, but disappearing all the same. the gazelles she had watched with such admiration for their sleek beauty had long since gone. eventually even the few remaining giraffes had meandered away. and she was left alone to amuse herself in the stodgy watering hole. even the trees were looking like they too wisht they could pack up their roots and go somewhere cooler. their leaves had fallen and even the sturdy branches were withering as the sun continued to scorch the earth.

one day during a particularly long and hot nap, she dreamt
the river had hardened around her to the point where it
was no longer even a river but just a flat bed of mud in
which she was encased. when she awoke she found she
could not move as she had dreamt in her sleep, and just her
wide nose and bulging eyes were left to look at the parched
land as the sun drove more and more moisture away.

THE BRAVE MOLE

over and over, handfuls of earth being moved from before
her to behind, the little mole worked digging slowly and
carefully, scratching soil away from the larger rocks that
marked her slow progress. roots of all sizes touch her skin
as she passes. she had left a trail of them that form sturdy
cilia within the womb of her tunnel. working a space big
enough to turn around in, she turns back to view her work
and is pleased that she has come so far in such a short time.
she stops and lets herself rest a while as a reward, thinking
just a bit further and i will be far enough ahead to raise my
hands straight above me instead of having to dig through
all these rocks and roots.

though she is tired, she is too excited to rest for very long.
she sets about digging as quickly as she can, leaving mounds
of the sweet earth in trails behind her. her arms ache but
she cannot stop. finally, taking a last handful, she sees the
light of day. it is blinding as she thought it would be. but
blinking a few times in the brightness, she turns this way
and that to feel the yellow-green grass surrounding her and
smell the apple-red roses. her whiskers twitch in nervousness, but she steadies them, spreading them to their fullest

to sense her new surroundings. the trees are translucent giants towering above her. they seem so tall she flinches, thinking how easily they could topple over with nothing solid for the branches to hold on to. the air tastes spacious and strangely warm. she breathes very quickly and feels once more her aloneness. terribly frightened but very alert, she pulls herself out of the ground she has come from and takes her first step in this delightful land.

THE RABBIT WHO WOULDN'T

the rabbit foraged in the earth for something sweet and tender to eat her front paws working quickly and deftly trying to get at the carrot. just a bit more dirt and i'll have it. oh how scrumptuous, she thought, her mouth watering.

earlier that day she had visited her cousin already married and two litters down another on the way. it had been so boring hearing her mother and aunt and relatives talk of babies and breastfeeding and what was the best way of doing what. she thought she would go mad hearing the same opinions she had heard so many times before. she had left early and had not eaten lunch. she knew her mother thought it very rude of her to leave so abruptly but it was better to forage in silence under the clear blue sky than listen to their incessant chatter. it wasn't that she minded them doing what they wanted but she felt claustrophobic in their atmosphere; she felt their expectations including and enclosing round her. she imagined her soul being eaten alive, drained completely while everyone sucked.

and it wasn't even that she didn't like children or mothers.

on an individual level when she saw them separately it was nice. they talked and had a rapport. but when the women of the family gathered together, she cringed and felt a complete outsider. maybe it was the group pressure. she had even gotten to the point where questions about why she was not pregnant yet made her burn and want to scream and hit the person who asked again this time. but she tried to appear calm and just shrugged or tried to laughingly say, not me. but she felt that she was immensely different and began to notice even the slightest changes in appearance and mannerisms that would single her out. she imagined her fur was growing a slightly different color than it used to be, slightly darker than the others. yet she was sure, rationally, that it was not. she riveted her attention on her tea cup in order to distract her mind from her thoughts. she took more tea. yes thank you, it was a lovely day.

perhaps it had been worse today because she had been so hungry, she thought as she munched on her carrot. "you mustn't let these emotions get the best of you—they are the past. if you really aren't going to have children, then don't worry about it. there's no law that says you have to." and as she said these commonplace things to herself she felt a sense of profound release. it was all so simple really, she just didn't have to do it.

THE ALL-ENCOMPASSING CLOSET

the young moth thought all this talk about fire and bright lights rather silly. she didn't have any desire to throw herself at anything that burnt bright and she'd seen quite a few things in her day even if she was still considered a child.

though that's what she kept hearing, what was whispered in corners and tetes-a-tetes and she knew it was what everyone would eventually expect of her. oh, in ways she could understand it. intellectually, that is. there was an attraction for its courage and brazenness and with her multi-faceted black eyes the fire burned brighter every time she looked and glowed in after image round her when she looked away. she wondered what the image might feel like if she were to go just a little closer and touch it. she shivered at the thought.

but these were mere fanciful musings, were nothing compared to the tremendous pressure she felt coming from her parents and even her peers. the excitement grew each day as one after another of the moths tested and battled the flame. ah, but she was not going to waste herself. while everyone talked, she looked for a dark closet full of coats and wools to hide in. when the time was right she would go and shut herself off from this lunacy forever. and maybe someday, when she was older and stronger, when she was first greying but still had the furry orange eyes marked on each wing, she would return in all her stubborn glory. perhaps a few of her friends would be left though their antennae would probably be singed, their eyes milky white, their wings frayed from fighting the dragon fire. then maybe she could convince them to join her and if she could, they would start a new strain of moths who didn't need fire to prove themselves with.

MOCKINGBIRD SEASON

the cats were tending to stay in the houses these days.

every time they went out a small but fearless mockingbird would swoop to pocket a beak-full of fur. the cats were one mark of bald patches from their unsuccessful attempts to remain outdoors in mockingbird season.

the mockingbirds waited on the wire leading to the house extending wings full measure as they dove when any cat emerged. they cawed like banshees screaming in the air.

but the moon brought out another side of the birds, perhaps one too that was related to the banshees. the mockingbirds for yards around sung on full moon nights. their chorus built as the moon waxed each month rising to a joyous clamourous exaltation of its round radiance. yet perhaps they only cried at those times to heighten the tension of the cats whose spatial and spiritual domain they had conquered.

whatever their reasons, they feathered their nests with the soft warm fur while their young grew stronger each day and even less afraid then they.

The Three Bears

Ruth Babcock

Lavinia was the eldest, forty-six, an earthy, slightly stout woman with thick dark hair. Margaret was forty-four, taller, thinner, with a pleasant face and hair not so dark or so thick. Judith was the baby, only thirty-eight, the tallest and thinnest. She had short blond hair. Lavinia and Margaret had husbands and children. Judith was a lesbian. She had always been frank about it with her sisters, who accepted it fairly well once they got used to the idea.

The three of them were alone together for the first time in many years and they were deep in a discussion of things both inconsequential and consequential.

"Vin," said Margaret, "you have as much hair as ever, and not a single gray one. Look at all the gray in mine. I really envy you that mop."

"Huh," said Lavinia, "I'd rather have less hair on top if it would mean less all over."

"Oh, that," said Margaret. "All three of us are stuck with that."

"And all because dear old Pa was a grizzly bear," said

Judith. "He should have had three sons instead of three daughters. He'd have been the first to agree, of course—not that he ever saw us nude."

"Rampant pubic hair from hip to hip," said Margaret with a sigh.

"A bushy line up the stomach to the navel," said Lavinia sadly.

"Hair on the chest," said Judith, "and fur on the legs. It's all Pop's fault. I remember when we were kids and the whole family would go to the beach on Saturdays. When Pop was in a bathing suit people would turn around and look at him."

"And giggle," said Margaret. "He looked like a rug."

"Two-inch hair all over his shoulders and back," said Lavinia.

"Say!" said Judith suddenly, "how did your husbands react to this?"

Lavinia lit a cigarette. "Before I was married I was using a safety razor, and I was always terribly clumsy with it. I mean, what other bride can you think of who went to her wedding with a cut on her chin from shaving? Then after we were married that creep Daniel was always making remarks about my five o'clock shadow. The nerve! His chin was purple—even after he shaved. Mine wasn't anything like that. Then he gave me an electric razor for Christmas and it got positively cozy after that—standing in the bathroom and shaving together."

Margaret and Judith laughed, and then Margaret blushed slightly.

"When Rex and I were going together," she said, "we didn't neck very much at first—but I knew that sooner or later he'd stick his hand inside my bra and I really dreaded it."

"Well?" said Lavinia, "And did he?"

"Of course," said Margaret. "I couldn't see his face but he gave several hairs a little tug and said, 'Shall I tease you?' I said, 'No!' and he didn't—at least not until we were married." She sighed and made a wry face. "The worst of it was, he didn't have a single hair on his chest."

"I suppose being hirsute hasn't cramped your style any, Judy?" said Lavinia.

"Not in the long run, no. But Migg's story reminds me of something that happened very early on. I was only seventeen."

Lavinia and Margaret leaned forward expectantly. They enjoyed hearing accounts of Judith's experiences, particularly since they were always shocked by them.

"When I was a freshman in college I fell madly in love with another girl in the dorm, and it was quite mutual. That was Bev; you might remember her name."

Both sisters looked blank.

"Bev and I were so close that her parents got worried because she wasn't going out with boys, and in the middle of a semester they took her out of school and sent her to a college back east. For the last three nights before she left I went to her room and got in bed with her for a while. We had to be awfully careful because the rules were strict and the house mother was always snooping around."

"I remember that nosy old bag," said Lavinia.

"She caught me climbing in the window one night. Well, I suppose you two really lived it up."

"On the contrary," said Judith, "we were seventeen, totally unsophisticated and inexperienced. We'd been in bed together before but except for general embracing we'd never touched each other below the neck. Oh, maybe around the waist, but never between the neck and the waist, and anything below the waist was unthinkable."

"Well, what was allowed?" said Margaret.

"Lots and lots of hugging and kissing. It goes without saying we never took any clothes off. We were very tender. The whole thing seemed sort of sacred to us, even when our insides were churning. We looked at each other a lot and uttered many words of love.

"Well, now that Bev was going away, we were in absolute despair. The first of those last three nights we lay in each other's arms, crying and kissing and declaring that we would die without each other."

"Ah, youth," murmured Lavinia.

Judith smiled. "The second night was different. I slid in on Bev's right side again and we clung to each other. But after some kisses and tears we lay on our backs, sort of facing each other and stroking each other's hair and cheeks. Then, breathlessly, we began to stroke shoulders and arms, and almost simultaneously we each laid a hand very gently on a breast—my left and her right."

"Do you have to be so specific?" said Margaret.

"Yes. You'll see. Once we got there we were practically paralyzed. We couldn't breathe or move or speak.

"Finally after a while I raised up on one elbow, leaned over and very lightly kissed her right breast—through her pajamas, of course. Then I lay down and she just as lightly kissed my left breast, also through my pajamas. Then in a complete daze I got up and went back to my room."

"But you had one more night," said Margaret.

"Right. And just before I went to Bev's room the third night I very carefully shaved all the hairs off my left breast."

Lavinia snorted, "Oh, come on Judy—"

"Yes, I did," said Judith. "The left one. And that night we got to where we'd left off the night before, and after a while I delicately, oh so delicately lifted her pajama top and kissed her right breast very lightly. And then she delicately lifted my pajama top and kissed my left breast. Then we covered up and lay on our backs all speechless and quivering. We felt that our love had been completely consummated. When we could speak again we whispered that we would belong to each other forever. Then we clung together and cried, and I went back to my room."

"Honestly, Judy," said Margaret, "do you expect us to believe that you shaved only one side?"

"So help me, that's exactly what I did."

"But how could you be so sure she wouldn't touch the other one?"

"I don't know. I've never been that sure of anything since, but I knew positively that she wouldn't."

"Well, what if she had? How would you have felt?" asked Margaret.

"I'd have died of embarrassment. At that time in my life I felt like a freak."

"Then I just can't believe you would take such a chance," Margaret said. "It would have been so easy to shave them both."

"Why bother?" said Judith, "when I knew what was going to happen?" She laughed and stood up. "I have to leave," she said. "I have a date with someone who loves every hair." She kissed her sisters and went to the door.

"By the way," she said just before she went out, "her name's Bev."

Puddin

Norma Stafford

When I was a child we had an old Jersey cow that gave unbelievable quantities of milk. Her name was Puddin, and in Mama's words, "She helped raise our family." Puddin was ever so gentle. Mama and I would go to get her in the afternoon at milking time. As soon as Puddin saw Mama, she would head towards us. When she reached us, Mama would swing me up on that soft yellow broad back, and I would ride Puddin home. I have always thought that Mama really felt close to Puddin.

In the summertime, Mama would sit on the ground in the barn lot to milk Puddin. While Mama was gathering that bountiful supply, she would make the surrounding hills ring as she lifted her beautiful soprano voice to sing "Amazing Grace." It took only a minimum amount of food to get Puddin to stand still through those milkings. In the late spring and through the summer, there would always be a pile of delicious fresh beans, pea hulls, or tender corn shucks for her to chomp on while Mama milked. Puddin dearly loved these delicacies, but try as I might, I could never eat them like she did. The above mentioned goodies are the reason that Puddin hurt Mama one time.

Mama had brought an arm load of fresh corn to the barn lot for us to shuck. Two of my sisters, Magdalene and Lorena, Mama, and I, proceeded to shuck the corn. We piled the shucks on the fence to give Puddin at milking time. That time came, but Mama sat down to milk and forgot to give them to Puddin. Puddin looked up and saw her shucks on the fence, and she just walked right over Mama, stepped on Mama's ankle and foot, knocked over the milk pail and went to her shucks. Mama let out a piercing scream that brought the entire family flying out of the house. I was sitting on the fence, yelling at the top of my lungs, cause at the ripe old age of three years, I was very much a Mama's baby.

Dad helped Mama into the house, checked her foot and said it was broken. He straightened the foot and bound it. Somebody finished the milking. I cannot remember who finished supper. The entire family was paralyzed because Mama was out of working order. She never saw a doctor, nor was she angry at Puddin, but that foot gave her trouble for as long as she lived. Mama was up the next morning using two straight-back chairs to support herself while she cooked breakfast. She would slide the chairs, one on each side of her, support herself on the chair backs and swing herself forward on one foot. She hopped around like that till Dad got her some crutches.

Milking time was an everyday must. Puddin had to be milked about four o'clock every morning, and just before supper every night. Milking time started and ended the day. I think for my Mama it was a time of much needed solitude. I remember her saying that milking time was the best time in the world to cry. She said sometimes it just felt good to lay her head against Puddin's warm flank, and let the tears roll while she milked. It would embarrass Mama to no end if she overslept and daylight caught her still milking. Dad or one of us kids would milk occasionally. Usually Mama milked Puddin herself.

When Puddin would show up with a new calf, Dad would say, "She dug it up." Once I was with Dad while he was clearing new ground for planting. He kept a close watch on me trying never to let me out of his sight. I slipped off into the edge of the woods. It was cool and dark in the woods and the thick leaves were soft under my bare feet. I was absorbed in stepping on those leaves, and watching my feet disappear under them. I walked a little ways like that and suddenly, I almost stepped off into a huge sink hole. I stared at the hole a few seconds, then spun around and ran to get my daddy. Years later he would laughingly tell of an excited child, as she showed him the hole, "Where Puddin dug up all those calves."

Puddin stayed with our family for twenty years. Except for the times she was pregnant, every two years or so, she never failed to keep us well supplied with milk and butter. When she was twenty years old, she had a baby and went crazy. Dad watched over her for two solid weeks. Mama did everything she could think of trying to help her, but Puddin never did recognize either one of them. She wouldn't eat, and wouldn't claim her baby so it could eat. She just hobbled around the barn lot bellowing in that mournful pitch that cows use when they have something too heavy to bear. Puddin cried like that night and day. I tried to get to her, but she couldn't see me and almost stepped on me. Whatever had gone wrong with her life was terrible. While she hobbled around and cried, I sat on the fence and cried. Mama and Dad finally got in touch with the glue factory people to come and get Puddin and her baby. Her baby didn't act right either. Besides, without Puddin there would be no milk to feed it.

Mama and Dad thought they were going to be slick. They didn't want me to know that Puddin and her baby were going away, but I overheard them talking about it. The morning that the glue people were to come for Puddin and her baby, Mama took me down to Aunt Matt's house. They kept trying to find things to occupy me in the back of the house. I kept running back to the front yard to stare down the dirt road for the glue truck. Eventually a cloud of dust announced the truck's arrival. We watched as that big ole truck rattled and rumbled into the barn lot.

I don't know how they got Puddin into that truck, but when they came back by Aunt Matt's house, she looked like she had always been standing there with her baby by her side. We three were standing in the front yard. As the truck went by I noticed something about Puddin. I grabbed Mama's hand and said, "Look, Mama! Puddin is finally letting her baby suck. Mama, Puddin has claimed her baby." My Mama sounded like she was choking and uttered a low, "Oh my God," as the truck rolled out of sight.

We had other cows after Puddin. It took a long time to find one that was worth a darn. I don't even remember if we ever named the cows that followed her. After she left, Dad would milk in the afternoon unless one of us kids wanted to. From then on, the milking always took place in the barn. You never can tell how a strange cow might act, so it's better to play it safe and have her in a milking stall. We never did have another cow that made Mama want to sing "Amazing Grace."

It's Hard to Stay Dry
in the Ocean

Helle

yes your allowed to moan and cry scream and hit your head
against the silence, go ahead but you cant run away
or forget or become fucked up- you have to survive
cause your a woman and you have a child and you have
to survive for her.
and every time you face a further in justice you just
scream some more hoping you wont be able to ever again
scream or cry again.

the friendly psuedo- intellectual phony liberal skulks
around on welfare check day announcing all businesslike
while eating home cooked rolls, well you know im still
the landlord and the rents are due today,
after he has just told you a couple of days ago he just
sold the house and everyone must move as soon as possible.
in the meantime, please pay the rent, if the rent gets
paid on time, he will refund the balance to you.
while he is 40,000 richer and is buying a vw camper new

from the dealer so he dont have to stand in line for
registration.

and he knows i am on welfare with a little girl to
support feed clothe pay rent on 148 a month
and when she needs new shoes i go to the rag pile on Hate St.
or force her to wear shoes too small for her feet,
and if i pay him the rent i have no money left to
find a place or to move with and the same story next
month, etc. and i know he dont give a damn,
and he knows how hard it is to find a place
on what i get from welfare, 58 a month is sf
and im tired of living on haight street in
free loving communes where all that is free are
the roaches and the police raids, and fear of being
ripped off for babys milk or what you have left
of your sanity and worries of being busted because there
are ten junkies nodding in the next room and the room down
the hall has two runaways under age and the hells angel
freak who thinks dracula visits her at night warns me
under lemon lime that we are all going to get busted
and charged with statutory rape or at least contributing
to a minor even pregnant madonna pandora who cries
for a lost virgin.
and the guy down the hall is dealing as is every one in
the house, and the alcoholic 50 year old hippie shows
two huge monstrous scabs on his hand that have swollen
into purple pus filled fungi and tells me casually he was
bitten by some scorpion in the room masika and i sleep now
our mattresses on the floor, and just be careful
so i lay awake at night with the lights trying to keep
masika from the walls, for even though he told me it might

not be deadly, its sure the hell painful and takes months
to heal,
and this is my haven that i found after searching for
days carrying masika who had a bad   and fever
and i was just in the middle of t   and pus on
the tonsils and did not know why   t and weak
and then chills and i thought i w   ie
but didnt go to uc, cause i thou   a cold
and if i kept taking aspirins
masika was crying and sick and w   o sleep
and my old mans was in langely por   es with
the doctors so he had a place   hen we
had no food we would wait in the   bill
finished eating and when i woul
food for masika to sneak off bil   ould not
eat, the nurse said it was against   f he
did not finish his food it would ha   n
away, and when i asked to lay down   o rest
they said it was not allowed and i   o
comfort bill because i thought he wa
destroy himself because, because i   fault
because i had nagged him and asked him   the
dishes or to help me survive and i thoug   had fucked
up his masculinity, for he had to baby sit while i went
to work in motel making beds and fucking old withered hairy
smelly old men to make money to pay the rent and to get high

any ways i felt guilty, meantimes i had no place to stay
bill took the easy way out by going into the hospital,
and our landlord changed locks on me without no
30 day notice, not even a 5 day notice.
so i spent what money i had left for the place on haight.

(See page 12 of the Introduction for an explanation of what's "wrong"
with this page.)

before that i was living at hunters point project
while bill was in the hospital and catching long buses in
the rain while both masika and me were sick.
living in hunters point with a beautiful young woman
named yvonne, a soft gentle person, whose baby of 8 months
smiled at her, the babys body badly scarred by burns,
and her old man who did not want any one to know he was
not the father of the baby, but under the name of discipline
would always be spanking that 10 months old baby girl,
and not allow her to be picked up and played with, he
would spank the baby for crying, to make the babys bladder
loose, etc.   and then come to my room and politely
tell me i am not disciplining my child enough while
i pay my own rent and food, the court had tried to take
the child away because neglect for the burns but had not.
later i found marcus gave up the baby to yvonnes mother
for now they had their own baby a son. who was his.
so the loss of my innocence again happened each day
as i walked the bastard streets of nyc, 47 th st and bwy
with masika in my belly and fucked garlic old men
musky funky hairy as they coldly accented suck my dick
lick my balls, you like quick fuck and ten measly dollars
and then scared i would run home with my loot and buy
food, and next day the perfumed powdered businessman who
for 15 would want you to lick hiss ass and lick his
whole hairy body concentrating on the shaved balls
and tell you to squeeze them HARD, hard . . . . .
and next day the pipsquicked looking paranoid
who promises you alot and gets you a taxi, so
with swollen baby stomach you think itll save
all those subways and six flights of stairs to
walk and im 7 months and its getting hot in august in
nyc, so i go and in the taxi, he keeps trying to grab you
and feel you and poke his finger in you and rub his sandpaper

skin on your cheek all in the back seat of a taxi, and then
later gives you only ten, but you think ill just grab
that and get rid of him and he cant get a hard on and wont
and you try like a sonofabitch licking that hairy belly
and cock cause thats what your getting paid for, so
you do it automatically ignoring disgust and the smell
the hair in your mouth any dead roaches you might find
there feeling the wet mucous from his dick and if hes
not circumcized the dirt and mucous and old toilet paper
that can be rotting beneath those folds rotting red
dick, that wont get hard and he tells you to
jerk him off, hell come right away, why didnt he tell me
that before, and you jerk till you hand falls
off and aches and its no harder, and i give up as he
says why dont you try licking my ass, that always
works, and when i tell him thats it to get out
he, no longer meek old man hits me and grabs my purse and
leaves, luckily i never put my money in my purse
but hide it any place as soon as i get it, in the toe of
my shoe, etc. and always get the money first.
and that was just one day . . . .

what i wanted to say, i wish someone could understand
and care, there is nothing about life and men and
people i havent been through, i will not go through
it again, ive been loved raped lied to deserted wooed
beaten, seen the greed on a crippled hustlers body
when he looked at me and only saw the money i might
be able to produce for him to become famous and
threaten my life, and have to run in the night with my belong-
ings in a paper bag trying to escape,
and on and on- what did you think a pimp, hustler, whore
money money life was like----------

Shoes

Pat Parker

"Gal, don't you ever do that again. You hear me?"

"Yes, daddy."

Victor released his daughter's arm and laid down his belt. Frances ran off to her room. She could hear her father still raging to her mother.

"That girl's gonna cost me all my jobs. Mr. Clark said she was down right insolent to him on the phone. She's got to understand that white folks don't like being talked to like that. They decide that she's too uppity and that reflects on me. They'll stop calling and then what'll we do."

"Now Victor, calm down. She's young. She don't understand yet about these things."

"Well, dammit! She better start! It don't hurt nobody to say yessir to nobody. That girl is just too smart for her own good. Hell, she talks to me sometimes like I'm a child. All those damn teachers and books are getting to her head."

Frances turned over in her bed. She was angry. She had not done anything wrong. She had answered the phone; told the man that her father wasn't home. She'd written down his name and number, said good-bye and hung up. The only thing she hadn't done was to punctuate her sentences with sirs. Why was it so important to say sir? That was for people you respected a great deal. She didn't even know the man on the phone. For all she knew he could have been a drinker or gambler. Anything. She ran her fingers over her body. She could feel the sting from the belt and trace the outline of the welts beginning to form. But she didn't cry. No matter how long and hard he hit her she wouldn't cry. And she knew that got to him. I can't stop him from whipping me, but I don't have to cry. And that gets him everytime. She smiled at the thought.

Victoria cries if daddy looks at her funny. And Janice and Reba will cry if he whips them, but not me. She was tougher than any of her sisters and she was the youngest. I'll never let him see me cry.

She had come to know her father well in her ten years. In the summer, he would often take her to work with him. They moved from used car dealer to used car dealer. He would drag his six foot frame from his car and put on his smile. "Howdy do, Mr. Whoever. Need any tires cut today?" And they would pause. "Well, Victor, lemme see. Yeah, I think we got a few over in the shed. Go on over and see Mr. Whoever." He would smile his grateful smile, take his stool and retreading iron and go find Mr. Whoever. While he worked she would amuse herself by climbing among the stacks of old tires. And when she tired of that, she would find an old magazine in one of the showrooms and sit and read. Some days there would be many tires and she would go get in her father's car and pretend she was some rich person, or an outlaw escaping from jail. Some days she would be a rich king, or a lonely rich boy with no parents. Or she'd be on a big ranch with as many horses as a person could have.

At least once a month, her father would decide that he'd earned enough money to take care of the family and they would go fishing. She loved to go fishing with her father. When she was eight, he had bought her her own rod and reel. Now instead of sitting on the banks with a line and old meat hoping to snare a crab, she got to sit on the banks with him and fish like the grownups. Sometimes they took the rest of the family. She didn't like those times. Her sisters and mother would complain all the time about going home. When she and her father went alone they would stay all day and well into the night.

Those were the good times; but she also knew her father on the days when there were no tires to cut. Then the house was silent with the fear of his rage. The chickens and rabbits were inspected very carefully. If the animal's water seemed the least bit yellow, she would be whipped. Any little thing wrong and his belt would be off his waist, wrapped around his hands and flying through the air at his target. She had seen him and felt him whip her and her sisters until her mother had grabbed him. Seen her mother stand painfully by and watch until he seemed out of control and then take him into the bedroom to find the man again. And she had learned not to cry. She was whipped more often and longer. His face would contort and his words would shatter sanity, but she would not cry. And her mother would stop him and she would lead him into their bedroom, his shoulders slumped and his step heavy. She would stand and watch, her eyes glaring, standing very tall. She would not cry, and she was the victor.

There was a new store. The vacant building behind the green pole that served as a signal for the Pioneer Bus Line to stop and pick up the Black people and take them from one ward to another had been transformed into an ocean of shoes. Frances stood and peered in the window. The large cardboard figure of Buster Brown and Ty smiled back at her and she thought of the commercial. "My name is Buster Brown. I live in a shoe. This is my dog Ty. He lives in there too."

Red and Terry approached her. "Hey, Frances, let's some peg." "Naw, I don't want to." Red and Terry were her friends. Each day after school they would come to the bus stop and play games while waiting for the green bus to take them home. They couldn't play together in school. The boys and the girls were each sent to their respective parts of the playgrounds. Frances hated playing with the other girls. They didn't like to play football or baseball. They only wanted to play silly girl games and giggle. But after school, she could play what she wanted. If the ground was dry, they would produce little sacks of marbles, and fire missles into a crude circle to destroy their opponents. If the ground was wet, they would produce rusty pocket knives and play peg. They were good friends. They always returned each other's marbles, and they never tried to break each other's knives in peg.

This day she didn't want to play. She watched the man in the store put one pair of shoes here, another there. She had never seen so many different kinds of shoes. Her entire world of shoes consisted of brown and white saddle oxfords for school, black patent leather for Sunday, and sneakers for play. Here in this store were red shoes, blue shoes, white shoes, sandals, boots, grownup shoes, kid shoes, the high laced old lady shoes, all kinds of shoes.

"Hey, Frances, here come the bus." All the way home, Frances thought about the shoes. She imagined herself rich and having all those shoes in her house. She watched herself changing shoes every hour and then throwing them away. She would never have to polish shoes again. She would never have to take off a pair of shoes before she could play. She could run in the mud or water and not worry about getting whipped. She wouldn't have to have taps to keep them from running over. She spent the rest of that day feeling good. Tomorrow she would get to see the shoes again.

Frances stayed after school that day and helped her teacher clean the boards and check the desks and cloak room for forgotten articles. She knew that Red and Terry would be at the busstop wondering where she was. But she didn't want to see them. They would want to play some game. She would take her time and let them go home. Then she could look at the shoes. They wouldn't understand if she told them about the fantasies. They would laugh. It would be better if she just let them go home.

When she reached the busstop, they were gone. She walked to the window and looked in. She saw herself a great dancer on television wearing the blue ballet slippers. People stood up and applauded her performance, throwing roses on the stage. She took her bows and smiled.

"What are you doing?"

"Huh! Nothing . . . sir."

Frances looked up at the white man. She had almost forgotten, but the memory of her recent whipping swept across her mind. She had seen this man before. Yes, he was the man in the shoe shop. She smiled.

"What's your name, little girl."

"Frances, sir."

"You live around here, Frances."

"No, sir, I live in Sunnyside. I'm waiting for the bus."

"Sunnyside. That's a long way from here. You know how to go all that way by yourself?"

"Yessir. I do it every day. I'm a big girl now. I'm in the fifth grade."

"Would you like to come inside and look at the shoes, Frances?"

"Oh, yessir."

Frances couldn't believe what was happening. This had to be the nicest man in the world. She felt really important. It was almost like she was going to buy some shoes.

"It's almost time for me to go, so I'm going to close up the shutters, Frances. You go ahead and look around."

Frances walked slowly around the display tables. Barely touching first one shoe, then another. She would wear that shoe to the movie, and that shoe to the park, and that shoe to the rodeo, and that shoe to the circus and . . .

"Would you like to go in the back and see where we store the shoes?"

"Yessir."

Frances followed the man into the little room. She stopped inside the door and he turned and beckoned her to a small stool. She sat and looked around the room. There were rows and rows of boxes. It was more fun to see the shoes in the other room. She wondered if the man would give her a pair of shoes. He closed the door and turned to her.

"Do you like candy, Frances?"

"Yessir."

At first she hadn't noticed the man walk up to her. He had unzipped his pants and was holding a large red thing, stroking it back and forth. His eyes were funny looking, like he was nervous.

"Do you know what this is?"

"No, sir."

"Well, this is like candy, and I want you to suck it. And

when you're finished I'll give you a present."

Frances looked at the large red thing. It didn't look very much like any candy she had seen. It looked like a long, large, red mushroom. There was something white in the middle coming out of a hole. She looked at the man.

"Go on, Frances, suck it."

He tilted her head and pushed the large red thing into her mouth. It felt hard and much too big. And it didn't taste sweet at all like candy. The man had his hand around Frances' neck. His grip tightened.

"Suck it, up and down like candy."

Frances was frightened. She didn't know what to do. She didn't like this candy. She didn't like the way the man sounded. His voice was mean like her father's. She felt like she was going to throw up and was afraid she'd be beaten. All of a sudden the man let out a cry. He pulled away from her and she stared as white cream came spurting from the large red thing which was becoming smaller. She didn't know what to do. She knocked over the stool and backed away from the man. He had taken a handkerchief from somewhere and was wiping the red thing. He pushed it back into his pants.

"Now, didn't you like that, Frances?"

"Yessir."

"Tomorrow, after school, you come back and we'll do it again. But you mustn't tell anyone about it. It's our little game. Okay?"

"Yessir."

The man led Frances to the door. He reached in his pocket and handed her a quarter. He unlocked the front door and let her out.

"Now remember. It's our private game."

Frances didn't answer. She saw the green bus and ran to

it. She didn't like the game. She looked at the quarter clutched in her hand. She dropped it on the floor of the bus. She was very quiet that evening at home. Her mother checked her forehead to see if she had a fever. She went to bed that night and she did not think about the shoes.

The next afternoon after school, Frances talked Red and Terry into catching the bus at the next busstop. She told them the man in the shoe store would probably take their knives if they played peg in front of his store. They never played there again.

Masks & Mirrors

Nancy Green

"This is a place to lose all your faces." she said, nodding at Era.

"I want only to find myself." Era flipped back.

"As you wish."

Era looked at the other woman. A witch she decided—a withered hideous old witch. She shuddered. The other woman took note of Era's repulsion and grinned in grotesque delight.

"This way, my dear." said Era's witch-woman, leading her down the paisleyed hall to a large oak door. They entered into a dark dressing room. The witch-woman motioned at a veiled mirror.

"Gaze into the mirror and remove your reflections. Put them here, on the shelf. Later you can recover them. When you are absolutely naked, the velvet curtain (her bony finger pointed to a burgundy colored drapery across from the oak door) will part and admit you into your inner reality. Don't try to enter without discarding everything first," she warned in a solemn tone, "or you may never be able to return." She left Era in the small dark room alone, closing the door behind her.

Era saw nothing in the mirror—it was cloudy and opaque in the dimly lit room. There was only one tiny candle on a wall sconce, which flickered and wavered nervously.

Slowly she began to undress. Boots, levis, sweater, bra—starting from the bottom. She stared into the mirror again.

Diffuse light emanated from it. She saw a floating mask. It was barely visible, a sort of composite Hip-Rebel, a mild sneer and cold knowing authority mixed with contempt. The eyes were barely the size of pin-points, the mouth was a long slot that spewed ticker-tapes of rhetorical phrases. She lifted her hands to her face, grasped the mask and wrenched it away.

She gasped.

Underneath was an angry, screaming face . . . eyes in slits, nostrils widely distended, lips drawn back over bared teeth . . . a vicious, cornered animal. She ripped this mask away.

The light from the mirror glowed brightly as she tore off mask after mask—Wonder Woman—Noble Martyr—Big Mama —Con Woman—Tough Broad—Sexy Kitten—Cold Bitch— Daddy's Girl—Frightened Child—Whiny Brat, and on and on . . . until the masks were slipping off the shelf and spilling onto the carpeted floor.

It began to hurt, the closer she got to the raw. She cried out in pain, afraid to go on—the mirror showed her Big Baby —she ripped it off, shrieking in agony . . . revealing Courageous Clown.

Now she was very near the end.

She rested. She felt very young again, and quite exhausted. Her memory was gone—she barely remembered before the last three masks. She was living in the present, having shed the accumulated masks of years and years she was now down to her earliest, most primitive masks.

She tore off the remaining masks. She stood bleeding and raw. The pain throbbed for a time, then she was free. She looked into the mirror and did not recognize her Self. There was nothing that she could relate—even remotely—to what she was seeing in there, nor could she maintain an idea in her head long enough to concentrate on what it was she was seeing.

She lost interest in the mirror the moment the burgundy curtain parted.

She passed through the opening in the curtain and found her Self in the midst of a vast desert. Overhead the sun blared in a white light sky. There was no shadow, no shaded area anywhere—just endless miles of wave after wave of silver sand.

The brightness of the light was, surprisingly, not hot at all. It was warm, the wind blew soft and warm. She felt good. She raised up her arms, leaned back her head, closed her eyes and stretched, strained and relaxed.

She felt the sand move beneath her. She fell backwards slowly. She slid along, eyes closed, felt the sand cross over her, under her. She rolled. Rolled on the waves of sand, dry and fine.

She was moving. Being moved. Sliding. The sand was warm, soft like caresses, like abstract hands or solid breaths, gentle. Her body roused, her eyes were closed as if in sleep. Her body grew pink, swelled, became very warm—hot—wet and swollen. She lay there panting. Covered in a fine layer of silver dust.
She opened her eyes when the sand ceased its movement. Sat up into twilight. The sky was violent purple melting into gold streaked crimson. Sand peaks were soft blue edged in fine rippling lines of gold. The deep hollows between peaks were violet or black. Purple sky slipped down over red, stars emerged from a blackening horizon.

To her left stood a tent—she rose and approached it. It seemed to be made of silk and was striped, in the twilight, with rich magentas and gold. The tent was circular, and where the cone-shaped roof met the vertical wall thousands of tiny shreds of fabric fluttered in the wind. The open entrance spilled yellow light out onto the sand.

She entered.

She stepped onto thick and intricate Persian carpets. Filigreed brass lanterns hung from the coneshaped ceiling on long thin chains, spreading their golden light over the tapestried walls.

A bed of great down-filled cushions, covered over by a large white fur, plush and soft as snow fox, took up half of the room space.

Beside the bed stood a low ornately carved chest. A table had been laid upon it, plates of delicious fruits, sweet meats, honeycakes,—a silver flask of red sweet wine.

Across the room stood two alabaster vases filled with rose-scented oils and ointments. She applied the ointment to her dry skin, rubbing in a lingering fashion, taking time to feel the cool, the softening. Her talcumed body sucked in the oils, luxuriated and tingled under her soft massage.

When she finished, she went to the table and ate and drank her fill.

Satiated, she laid down on the soft fur. She sank deeply. Slept. The lights glimmered and went out.

The moon rose, passed over and dipped in the sky, reaching a silvery tongue across the carpets in the soft dark tent.

She barely woke. Saw the slender form of a girl in the doorway.

"I'm here," whispered the approaching silhouette.

"Ah yes. I always knew it was you." she replied hazily,

reaching up to touch. She found soft flesh, warm and yielding, narrow wrists and gazelle-like legs, the form bending over hers on the bed.

"Come next to me!" she cried. The girl found her way, lay next to Era, pressed close and began caressing. They caressed . . . it was like the sand or the warm breathing wind or the brush of peacock feathers. Their bodies grew warm, swollen and opened . . . arching and rolling . . . they came together, mouths together . . . fell together, in the dark, softly on foaming waves, lifted up and swallowed down and then brought up and round and round, gently whirlpooling . . . enclosed and in the sea, in the belly of the dark green sea, in the warmth of the foaming sea . . . down down, around to the deeps . . .

. . . to the black. Black warm and wet . . . she . . . they plunged . . . two intertwining eels . . . fell down slowly . . . wetness compressing to tubular darkness. They fell through a narrowing tube, pressed together, pressing against flesh barriers which melted, they sifted into each other . . . locked into each other. Warm, dark and secret they curled, they tightened they burst, burst. Burst the dark ocean in spiraling magenta and opened and spewed and rained, rained. Rained down the ocean, rained down the foaming sea, rained down the darkness; the tube had burst, had burst, had burst . . .

Era woke.

She was lying on the carpet of the dressing room, next to a withered crone. They were naked. Wet. Faintly vibrating.

"I love . . . I love . . . I love . . " Era began.

"You. I love you. You." Era continued.

"Me." the crone said softly.

"You." replied Era, touching her lightly.

"You." said the crone, stroking in return.

"Me." said Era. She hesitated. Her brow darkened. "Me. You?"

"Yes," sighed the crone. "Yes. Yes." She rose from the floor slowly, regretfully, and wrapped herself in a faded chenille robe. She walked to the oak door, turned to look at Era a long moment—inscrutably, silently—then turned, opened the door and walked out closing it behind her.

Era lay in wonderment. Her wetness felt like dew. She felt fresh and new and full. She felt tingling.

She rose and went to the mirror. The mirror was full of dark space of the universe, spinning stars and nebulae clustered in moving galaxies, all pressing outward to the rim, rim of time.

She picked up a mask. She did not note which order.

"It doesn't matter, they will just come off again." she thought.

She chose the least repulsive masks to apply at first. She did not want to wear very many, just enough to remember. But as she applied one mask at a time, the masks seemed to take over the selection of the following mask—it was as if each were only aspects of the same mask. They were heavy, unpleasant, uncomfortable.

They brought with them the years, the memories, the experiences of her life. She began to feel enclosed in them, trapped, and then connected to them. They brought weight. She cried. She wondered which mask it was that was weeping. She began to feel frightened. Which mask was which? She had them all mixed up somehow. Would she be lost in them?

She dressed in the clothes she had worn into the room. She looked into the mirror to see which mask . . .

. . . in the dim light of the room the mirror was opaque, milky. As she opened the oak door and passed into the paisley hall where the witch-woman waited in a long dark gown. Era adjusted what she hoped was her Business-Lady mask into place.

"Let's go," she said briskly to the older woman, who flitted a quick guarded glance at Era, then led her to the Exit.

"Well." started Era, her memory dimming, "Good-bye."

"Oh," replied the witch-woman half-smiling, "I wouldn't say good-bye. You'll be returning, I'm sure . . . "

Era shuddered and took hold of the exit bar.

"I doubt it." she said coldly, glaring at the other woman.

"Each time it's different"—the crone began, as Era opened the exit and stepped Outside,—"but it's always the same."

The door shut, cutting the sentence into a remnant.

THAT MESERABLE SCAR

Linda Marie

I RAN UP BEHIND HIM, QUICK AS LIGHTNING AND STABBED HIM AND STABBED HIM AND AGAIN STAB* BED HIM SO'S THAT WAS ONE BLOODY SONAVABICH WHEN I GOT THRU WITH EM. PASTY DEEP RED BLOOD GUSHED AND OOZED FROM THE PARTS OF HIS BODY I'D JUS FINISHED STABBIN. I PULLED THE ROPE FROM UNDER MY PARKA AND TIED HIS LEGS TOGETHER, AN BEGAN DRAGGIN EM****SINGLE HANDEDLY THRU THE SNOW. I CLEANED MY KNIFE AND STUCK IT BACK INTO MY BELT. HE'D BE FROZ* EN BY THE TIME I GOT BACK TO THE CABIN***SHIT!! HE DESERVED IT****THEY'RE ALL THE SAME **RAPIN STEALIN MY FOOD KILLIN. SHIT! THEY ALL DESERVE IT.

I HEAVED THE BODY ONTO THE BACK OF THE SLED THEN ORDERED THE DOGS TO MUSH. IT WAS DUSK****SOON THE SUN WOULD LEAVE AND RE* TURN FROM THE SAME SPOT, THEN BOUNCE A* CROSS THE SKY. THAT WOULDNT BE FOR SEVERAL

MONTHS. THE SNOW STILL LAY HEAVY AND THICK ON THE GROUND. JAGGED EDGED MOUNTAINS SURROUNDED ME REMINDIN ME TO STAY STRONG TO SURVIVE THE ELEMENTS.

I ROAD ON THE BACK OF THE SLED WITH THAT MESERABLE CORPES STRETCHED OUT BEFORE ME AND THE DOGS RAN AHEAD OVER THE FROZZEN GLOSSY SNOW WE REACHED THE CABIN SHORTLY AFTER DARK. I DRAGGED THE BODY**THAT WAS NEARLY FROZEN, INSIDE. I GAVE THE DOGS THERE FREEDOM AFTER WORKEN ALL DAY AND THREW THEM SOME MEAT***THEY NEVER ASK FOR MORE THAN THAT. I'D WORK EM LIKE CRAZY SOME DAYS AN THOSE ASS HOLES WOULD BE HAPPY AT THE END OF THE DAY JES GETTIN FREED AND HAVIN MEAT THROWN TO EM.

I LIT UP THE COLMAN LANTREN AND THREW MORE COAL IN THE STOVE**A LITTLE MORE WOOD AND STOOD OVER THAT GODDAM BODY***GOD* DAM PLEASED TO BE A STRONG HEALTHY WOMAN AN STANDIN OVER A DEAD MALE I'D JES BRUTAL* LY KILLED.

I SAT ON THAT STOOL I GOT AN OPENED THAT FUCKERS LEGS AND BEGAN PULLIN AT HIS BALLS ****JES WONDERIN IF I OTTA CUT EM OFF FIRST. I PULLED OFF MY PARKA AND TOSSED IT IN THE CORNER OF THE ROOM THEN UNFASTEN THE KNIFE FROM MY BELT. HADA NOTHERON IN MY BOOT ***BUT HARDLY EVER USED IT. I GRABBED THOSE BALLS UP IN MY HAND AGAIN AND CUT SLOWELY THE SKIN THAT WOULD SEPERATE THEM FROM HIM. I HELD HIS BALLS OVER HIS HEAD. YEAH I HELD THEM OVER HIS HEAD AND SAID****LOOK

WHAT I DID TO YOU SONAVABICH!! AH! I FIGURED
HIS SPIRIT MUSTA BEEN GOIN CRAZY BOUT THEN.
I WENT TO THE DOOR AND THREW THAT MEAT
TO MY DOGS. I SAT BACK DOWN ON THE STOOL
AND WATCHED THE BLOOD OOZ FROM BETWEEN
HIS LEGS. I DONT SUPPOSE I COULD BE THIS WAY
DOWN IN THE STATES***NO ONE UP HERE TO TELL
ME WHAT TO DO. WHOLE LOTTA MALES DOWN
THERE KILLIN***RAPIN***ROBBIN***GOTTA WAIT
FOR SOMEONE ELSE TA DO SOMETIN ABOUT IT.
I RESTED MY ELBOWS ON MY KNEES THEN LIFT*
ED MY HAND TO MY FACE AND RAN MY THUMB UP
AND DOWN THAT MESERABLE SCAR LEFT BY A FE*
MALE****MAYBE THIS ONES SISTER??? I HOPED
TO GET HER TOO ONE DAY.
I GORGED OUT THE EYES. THEN I GOT A NEEDLE
AND SOME STRING AND STRUNG THE EYES ON IT
AND HUNG THEM OVER THE DOOR. CUT OFF THE
HEAD NEXT. I STARTED AT THE THROAT AND CUT
AROUND TILL I GOT TO THE BONE THEN I GOTTA
HAMMER AND BROKE THE SONAVABICHS NECK
RIGHT OFF HIS BODY.
I PUT MY PARKA BACK ON AND WALKED OVER TO
THE DOOR WITH THE HEAD IN MY HAND. THE DOGS
GOT UP AND STARTED CIRCLING RESTLESSLY. I
BEGAN SWINGIN THE HEAD****THE DOGS WERE
GROWLIN AND GETTIN MORE RESTLESS WITH MY
TEASIN***I THREW THE HEAD INTO THE MIDDLE
OF THE PACK AND WATCHED THEM TEAR AND PULL
AT THE MEAT. I SQUATTED DOWN IN THE DOOR
WAY. A LIGHT SNOW WAS FALLIN AND THE YELLOW
LAMP BEHIND ME WAS FLICKERIN MAKIN THE SHAD*
OWS IN FRONT OF ME DANCE ON THE SNOW. THERES

AN EERI SILENCE HERE****THE DOGS SLURPIN AN GROWLIN WAS SO LOUD NOW.

COULDNT SEE THE STARS WHEN ITS OVERCAST LIKE THIS BUT GESUS THERE PRETTY WHEN ITS CLEAR, I KNOW WHEN I TALK TO THE STARS THEY CAN HEAR ME***ITS LIKE WE'RE ALL THAT IS ***YA/NO?

SHIT! YA SHOULDA SEEN THOSE DOGS TEARIN THAT HEAD APART! NOW, DOGS ER TOO STUPIT TO TALK TO***I DONT BOTHER SAYIN NOTHIN TO EM THATS NICE. THE MORE I WATCHED THE MORE I HATED THEM. ONE BIG BITCH FINISHED AND SAT PASSIVELY NEXT TO ME LICKIN HER LONG MOUTH. YOU STUPID BITCH I SAID, IF I CUT YER HEAD OFF AND TOSSED IT IN THE SNOW YER FRIENDS WOULD TEAR AT IT THE SAME AS WITH THAT OL' WOLFS HEAD.

Turtle Voices

Mary Jo McConahay

Rain splinters my view of the fisherman, his bare feet a
blur as they speed him to the far end of the beach. What are
they shouting, his woman and the children? I have trouble
with those words on the best of days. Now, this storm, the
shrill voices and the mountains of salt water exploding on
the rocks transform the language of the conquistadors to so
many mad muffled cries. They revert, that's what they do.
The Indians who fish these waters speak Spanish better than
I, but they revert sometimes. Odd syllables emerge then,
atavistic murmurings which threaten to rip open the fine
roll of their adopted castellano. When they are jubilant and
aroused, as they are now, watching the fisherman run, the
danger of total reversion to their native tongue is most
clear and present.

I cannot understand them for the surf in my ears, and
cannot see exactly what they see for the cactus liquor
shooting from my gut to my brain, then dribbling down
again over my eyes to blunt whatever perceptions the
natural elements may have left me. They are pointing. All
the others under the shelter with me are pointing, the
woman and the children and the two (also unintelligible)
Germans are pointing in the direction of the fisherman.
If only I can follow the line begun at the German's shoulder,
follow it down his khaki'd sleeve to the sunburned hand,
take it out to the pad of his stubby first finger . . . and this
is the hard part . . . concentrate . . . concentrate . . . Jump

it! Jump the space from finger's end to fisherman and sure enough . . . There he is, endlessly running in place, smaller, becoming smaller and smaller as the rain melts him and the sand swallows him up and the dry gallery in shades of brown cheers him on and on.

They are trying to explain to me, these good people are trying to explain to me exactly what is happening, what the man is running toward. I smile at the mouth but don't dare take my eyes from the moving speck.

The mezcal is finished. I raise the bottle to look up through its bottom, and pick at the worm with a strip of palm.

In the brown and purple village near Mexico City, Carrie hung on to the poets and painters of the foreign colony, and lived through them. The men she chose, and there were many, were hangers-on of a hanger-on. They were Mexican boys in a rock band, or young American businessmen who were headquartered south and spent weekends in the village for its climate and Bohemian reputation, or they were vacationing college teachers who saw the colony as an exotic coterie of non-conformists, living far from the real world alongside natives who still spoke the language of the Aztecs.

She wouldn't take the pill after her husband left her, over a year ago. She couldn't get pregnant, she said; she was sterile, she knew. All those men, all the time. She and Anna and I might go to a party, and Carrie would be with a man in five minutes, but really *with* him, taking him home in half an hour. At the cafe, often she couldn't sit still until some male friend joined our table. On Sunday nights that summer, we met at Stella's and the seven or eight of us women would eat, and make music, and speak softly, and march our private fears in front of each other until three or four in the morning when we raced for the big pond and swam under the dark cliffs where the Great Feathered Serpent was born. In August, when Carrie found out she was pregnant, she told us on a Sunday night. She talked for two hours, all by herself, then she laughed and cried at once and finally jumped up and stripped naked and said, "Let's go swimming, *now!*"

For awhile, Carrie stopped collecting men, and since she didn't need them any more, they seemed to like her better. She pulled out her twelve string quitar again, for the first time in months. On a Sunday night, she told us she once had her own show on Seattle T.V. and played her theme song. It was rusty, very rusty; but we knew it was still far superior to any of the other music we picked and tooted that night.

When Anna and I returned from Brownsville, we heard our friend had paid an enormous sum for an illegal abortion in Cuernavaca.

At Jose's party, someone else was playing her guitar, and Carrie sat in the kitchen eating men by candlelight.

The "doctor," they said, used belladonna to ease her spasms, and she hallucinated under the cheap potion. The dark man in white fragmented into a team of medical gardeners, all scraping out her womb with small hand rakes. She choked on her screams and they gave her large doses of caffeine, but the antidote was not enough. Carrie no longer needed the pill or any other control, she knew. As a woman she was incomplete. Her insides had been scoured dry and she told us she lost the mushy plumbing every woman needs to grow new life.

Deadly nightshade.

Running again, returning at a plodding run, the fisherman shoulders a flailing green burden. He'd spotted the turtle down the beach with the eagle eye of a man who must compete with other animals for his food. Jubilant, he is, jumpy and proud are the woman and their children. He puts the huge, mottled shell on a level spot and motions the Germans to stay back with their cameras and their loud talk. Only the youngest child continues to squeal and the Germans clack their shutters and speak matter-of-factly as if they had witnessed such scenes a thousand times and now only condescend to record the wonder for *Der Spiegel.*

And where did I read about turtles laying eggs? Perhaps it was in the telephone office in the village, waiting for the call to come through from New York. Yes, the ragged pocket magazine was vintage 1960, and on its cover was a great green turtle, like this one peeking a scaly head from under her shell. A female turtle will travel thousands of miles to find a special spot to lay her eggs, it said, a spot she knows by instinct, like radar in her womb.

I should have turned to the back where the story was continued.

Instead, I read the next article about a man who hadn't slept in twenty years, since his lover was killed in a London blitz. No doctor has been able to help the man, said the story, no cure for his eternal watching can be found. His bed is never rumpled, and for years his only solace was his all-night cigar stand near Victoria Station. When English law closed the kiosks between midnight and 6 a.m., he wrote to the Queen requesting special consideration. But the Queen refused. Even now I see the picture of the dear man, his dark eyes circled by well after well of sleepless gray. He's walking toward me now, the dreamless man is walking toward me and his thin lips curl into a zombie's grin.

"Will you have some more mezcal, senorita?" asks the fisherman.

If only I had read on about the turtles. Would I understand better what is happening here now? A green armored mother flicks sand into the air. The storm is breaking up and the turtle digs her deep sandy nest. I try to pry the cork from the new bottle but half of it gets pushed inside and blocks the neck so the clear golden stuff only trickles into my glass. I drink to the phone call from New York that never came through.

Susan wouldn't even tell me, her own sister, how it was at the end. She described the beginnings well enough; how she and Robby were walking down the Champs Elysee one sunny morning, still on their extended honeymoon, when she felt she was going to faint. They stopped for tea and then climbed the Eiffel Tower, where Susan vomited gloriously with all Paris at her feet. They fascinated me, those letters from abroad. I was awed by the experience of my little sister, married to a soldier and actually as pregnant as I can remember mother being pregnant with her. And she described the steps along the way, how it was hard to go to the bathroom sometimes, how this ached and that burned, how *paella* made her sick now and how wonderful it all was. Later I found out nobody believed her when she said she was ready, the doctor said, "Not until morning, at the earliest, my dear," Robby went home to sleep, the nurse turned off the lights. Mother always said she should have come home to have her baby, that she had no faith in foreign hospitals or army doctors (Daddy was a navy man), and that "we," meaning our female line back to great-great-grandmother giving birth in a wheat field outside Warsaw, always had trouble with our "firsts." The end for Susan was lonely, her cries ignored while her head burst and the bed was suddenly wet. When the nurse came in to give her a sedative, she found Susan straddling the bed with one foot on the floor, the sheets flung off, and little sister bending double to grasp the head tearing through the lips between her legs.

The rain has almost stopped now. The clouds are moving fast and low so the respite may be short. I won't get too wet if I walk from the shelter down the beach and around the point. If I can just wait for this wave to recede . . . But no, must get my feet wet after all and round the point quickly so I won't be sick in sight of the Germans. The Indian family doesn't care, but those Germans—they watch every-thing. Somehow I mind that they should know. The hazy sluice of the horizon still flows between them, but sea and sky are trading top and bottom. Not enough time to dig a little hole . . .

I cannot tell if I am sick from the mezcal or for the new life in me. The slimy product looks the same, doesn't it? I cover it with sand, like a good camper, and watch the pink crabs burrow in front of the wave.

Around the point again, I cannot walk back to the shelter. The sun is breaking through the clouds, the severe tropical sun which can suck up a tide pool in minutes. Already the rocks are dappled dry. It swabs the shine from the turtle's shell until only her eyes remain glistening. They glitter for the ordeal she is going through, the excruciating ordeal of birth which has carried her from a strange sea to this beach to that pit where egg after egg is born into a sandy nest. And all nearby, all save the mother are vigilant—all those unconcerned with the pain and decision of birthing are ready to pounce upon the new birth. The mouths of the fisherman and his family salivate in anticipation of the delicacy, the Germans reload their cameras. Flesh eating birds swoop low to survey the mother's progress. Standing on top of the shelter's roof, Katherine Hepburn wears Mrs. Venable's summer chiffon and whispers to me across the sand: "Sebastian guessed that possibly only a hundredth of one per cent of their number would escape to the sea."

In 1966, when such things were brave and rare, Esther didn't know or care who was the father of her child. And I, still an undergraduate, could say to my Anthropology T.A., "Yes, I have a roommate who doesn't know or care who the father of her child is." I was big on vicarious bravado those years.

Her family paid new attention, and I heard, for I had moved East by then, that the baby became everyone's business. She married, they said, for love, and divorced for her own reasons, after another child was born.

Last winter I went back to Berkeley and took the top floor of the house where Esther lived below with her two children. Always I'd remembered her midnight insights, her anger and self-knowledge, and recalled her as the most independent woman I knew. In a week my model was shattered, in a month the scene became painful to watch.

Can I say "she struggled to make ends meet" and have the words mean anything at all? For *struggle* in that house was a constant thing, a cohabiting monster, a river that flowed over the stone of Esther, hourly, daily, monthly, just as hard to escape, and causing erosion just as sure and permanent. Monthly she demeaned herself, begging Jamie's father for money. She stood in line for food stamps, waited long hours as clinics when one of the children was sick. Of necessity, she became a pest to the neighbors, begging babysitting here, rides there. A steady job was out of the question—the only kind she could get wouldn't pay transportation and someone to watch the children. Every few weeks I'd see her leave the house to work a convention or a trade fair, brochures under her arm and breasts spilling out of a peasant's blouse, or wearing a green lamé pantsuit with "A Better Idea" stitched on the butt.

That morning I heard her footsteps on the stairwell. "Come in, the door's open."

The big watchdog, Noodles, stood at Esther's side.

"Hi! Can I borrow some wax paper? It's *our* day at the Brownies'," she said, rolling her eyes.

At 2:30 the footsteps came again, fast and furious this time, and Esther burst in without knocking.

"That dog!" she trembled. "That damn dog! The cookies!"

The blond hair stuck out in coils, the blue eyes flashed dark and unbelieving. Her whole body was taut to the point of snapping.

"I walked to the store," she said, "for some sprinkles. When I got back . . . Noodles . . . he'd ate them all! All the cookies!"

Her look was so urgent, her words so comic, I didn't know which tack to take. Then she drifted away—her body stood there shaking, but I could see Esther herself slip away into some dark private vision of domestic horror and stress.

"I'll go with you," I said. "We'll buy some more."

"Don't you see?" she sobbed. The words came in clipped bunches. " . . . cost too much . . . need dozens and dozens . . . starts at three . . . home-made . . . show the other mothers . . . show Tina . . . I love . . . always . . . always . . . always . . . "

Uncontrollable now, on her knees, she tore at her skirt, the rug, the paper.

I grabbed her by the shoulders and shook her like a pillow.

"Esther . . . Esther! It's absurd. Overreacting. It's a simple daily crisis!"

She whimpered and eyed me curiously. I spoke more calmly, still holding her by the arms.

"You can't just crack up over some cookies."

"Over some cookies?" she whispered.

She bolted from the floor and began a macabre, screeching chant which I couldn't quiet: "Over-some-*cook*-kies . . . ! Over some-*cook*-kies . . . ! Over-some-*cook* . . . "

Emergency Mental Health Services was acquainted with Esther, so I didn't have to spend much time with forms. I arrived at the Brownie meeting to deliver three packages of Oreo's and two gallons of Hawaiian Punch, brought Tina home, collected Jamie from a neighbor, fixed them dinner and picked up their mother from the hospital. She was drowsy from the sedation they gave her, and when I checked downstairs at nine, I found the three of them, Esther and her children, asleep on the couch, inextricably wound up in a loving triangle before the flicking gray eye of their T.V. set.

From across the beach I see my turtle is finished. Her neck pivots from the shelter, to the sea, to me, and back again to the sea. She lingers over the eggs, gathering strength, and those under the shelter are patient: they know the fruit of her womb is theirs, that in the end she has no control.

When finally she begins her crawl down the beach, the fisherman brings a plastic bucket, allowing the Germans to come along this time. I walk nearer and watch the eggs, two by two, disappear from the nest. They are round, like golf balls, but the shells are smooth and thin. They appear fragile—I can almost see through them---but none break as they are counted into the bucket. Noventa y cinco, noventa y seis, noventa y siete . . . Ninety-eight eggs. I am astounded, but the fisherman frowns and says the number is not good at all, that he has found three times that many in a single pit. Nevertheless, he composes a victory face like an actor about to make an entrance, and swings to his feet, facing the shelter. The woman and children squeal and jump, but this time I do not even try to understand. The fisherman lifts the bucket with one arm and raises the other in salute, as if he had laid every egg himself. The turtle does not look back.

Cracked shell by cracked shell, I am jolted from the trance. The children suck the yellow mucous and giggle until it drips from their chins onto their little brown chests. The yolk dries to a dead crust on the woman's arms and her cotton apron, and still she digs in the bucket for another egg. The Germans feel superior to the gross habits of the natives as they snap away with their cameras. I grab my belly with both hands. Are you still there? Hang on, little egg, I've got you covered. *Rise up, my love, my fair one, and come away*. But I have never been brave, always I have been afraid of pain, of accountability. *For, lo, the winter is past, the rain is over and gone*. A dark cloud swings low, but the squall blows dry.

No one notices as I cross the beach to the road.

"Good-bye, family. Good-bye *meine Freunde*. I'm off to catch a bus."

The wind fills her nest with sand, and the turtle rides a wave out to sea.

The Last of the Weekend Visits

Kathryn Kendall

Sure enough, Harry was waiting for her in the San Antonio
bus terminal on Friday night. Fat old Harry, double chins,
flabby waddle, flat eyes. Even his fingers, she noticed as he
took her small suitcase, so fat the flesh bulged over the
knuckles. Same old fat Harry she had married and slept with
for three years. Pat-on-the-ass Harry.

"Are you alone?" she asked.

"Yep. The boys're watchin television. It'll be bedtime
soon. Seven-thirty already. Got any more luggage?"

"Yeah, this one's nothing but presents. Just a minute—I'll
go get the other one."

She joined the line at the luggage counter, knowing she
would have to wait till tomorrow to see Kevin. Twelve and
a half hours on buses and it would still have to be another
night. She'd fantasized possible scenes of meeting Kevin in
the bus station—with Harry, or with Harry's present wife,
Gloria, or perhaps with Gloria's eleven-year-old, John.
She'd worked out a script for every eventuality: the casual
one, "Hello Kevin, what's happenin?"; the tender one,
"Kevin. Oh Kevin, I've missed you,"; the defensive one,
"Well Kevvy, I see you've brought along the whole family,
huh?"

"The white one, yes. That's mine."

"Let's see your claim stub, lady."

She searched her handbag. Dramamine, checkbook,
change purse, can of Sucrets. She started piling things out

on the red formica counter top, sifting through the brushes, emery boards, pens and pencils. There were mutterings behind her. Her hands trembled. "It's gone. I can't find it. Well. Well, but I can tell you everything that's in there. A yellow sweater, a blue flowered nightgown, a pair of—"

"Hold it, lady. Hold on." He pulled out a clipboard with forms on it. She heard grumblings from the people behind. A cowboy-type with greased down hair said aloud,

"Goddam women. Can't hold a damn ticket an they wanna run the country."

"Name, Ma'am?"

"Carrie Kimbrough. K-i-m-b-r-o-u-g-h."

"Address?"

"4706 St. Charles Avenue, Apartment 8, New Orleans."

"Contents of the bag?"

Carrie ran through the contents again. Her throat felt tight, dry. She felt protective of her things, her blue flowered flannel nightgown Gran gave her last Christmas, all these people listening. It was like walking into the laundromat and finding someone had stolen your dryer-full of clothes. Those stained underpants, the bra with yellow straps. Violation of.

"Open it up."

Her hands trembling even more, damp now, she opened the battered high school graduation luggage, now ten years ole, revealing her very private soul, her flannel nightgown, right on top. The Greyhound man thrust his square red fingers into it, shuffled through her underware, fingered her blue shoes. "Yeah, O.K. You claim this as your bag?"

"Yes," she pulled the sweater over the nightgown, hastily, and snapped the case shut.

"Sign here. Next!"

Harry was chatting to one of the mechanics. He looked at his watch as she came out.

"What's the hold-up in there?" he accused her. With a sneer he showed he knew it was her fault. He knew her, Harry did.

She shrugged, smiled. "I don't know. You know these bus places." She looked at the mechanic, felt her face hot, looked away.

"So long, José. Don't work too hard now. Don't do anything I wouldn't do." Harry slapped him on the back. They winked.

Good old Harry. He always made a point of chatting with stock boys in grocery stores, gas station attendants, other people's yard men. Showed what a good guy he was. Soon as they were out of ear-shot of José, Harry mumbled, "Lazy goddam Mexican. Knock up their little Margaritas an collect my tax money for their bastards. Damn wetbacks, no wonder they love it here."

Same old Harry. Carrie felt the muscles in the back of her neck tighten. The stock boys love him. A real guy. He opened the trunk of the company car, slid her suitcase in, slammed it. She got in and pressed up against the door, wondering how she ever got herself into this. Watched Harry arrange himself behind the wheel. He burped. She could smell garlic. Christ. He lit a Kent and the old bedroom odor came back, acrid, suffocating. She rolled the window down and leaned her head out a little, looked up at the Little Dipper.

"Ramada Inn?" he asked.

"Yeah. I made reservations from New Orleans. I don't guess I can see Kevin tonight, huh?"

"No indeed. We can't destroy our schedules just cause you come to town, you know. Bedtime is bedtime. A kid needs rules. You've never understood that."

She tightened her hands into fists in her lap. Her voice came out flat, toneless: "Harry, maybe you don't know

209

what I understand and what I don't. A person can change a lot in four years. I'm a lot more than four years older."

He snickered. "New York'll do that for ya. You miss the Big Apple, now you're down south again, huh?"

"Not much."

"Had to have your shot at it, didn't ya? Always had to have a shot at makin it big. Biggest damn daydreamer I ever saw." He was looking for weak spots, probing, jabbing away already, grinning at his work.

"How's Kevvy?" Her voice sounded too high.

"Fine, fine. Gloria's got 'im in great shape. A real firecracker, that boy."

"He should have gone to school this year." She bit her bottom lip.

"Now look, young lady, don't you come here and start criticizin, you hear? It's the school system, won't let em in if they get to be six after September first. Now I told you that on the phone an you just keep your mouth shut about it, you hear?"

Young lady. Shit, she thought. Harry always acted like she was an undisciplined child. His eleven years had seemed awe-inspiring when she was 20 and he was 31. The year they got married. Now it was ridiculous. She could hear her breathing in the car, too loud, too obvious. She flattened her voice again, slowed it.

"September fifth. I just think you could have gotten him in."

Harry pulled the car over to the side of the road and stopped, his cigarette dangling from his lips. He turned sideways and seemed to blow up his chest so he completely filled his side of the car. Right was on his side, his son, he'd done all he could.

"Carrie, I'm onna turn right around an see you back to that bus station. Now you turn your bitchin off, you hear?"

Carrie looked out the window. She could feel her heart-beat shaking her whole body. Sweat ran down her left side. He started the car again and eased into the road. He kept going north. She breathed again.

They passed the zoo entrance and Carrie remembered last August, six months back, shen she came on a weekend visit. She had rented a car, then. She had been working in New York, making good money. She was engaged to Ian, planning to marry him and move to Scotland, and she was so much younger. Six months ago. It was long to the Ramada Inn.

Carrie fumbled for the lamp, looked at her watch: 4:25 a.m. She got up to use the bathroom. Her head ached, badly. She winced at the lights, wondered why motels always had fluorescent lights in bathrooms. They make your face look gray-green. Make all the little bumps show. She shuddered at her reflection, sat, holding her head, elbows on her knees, listening to the familiar sound of her own pee. Carrie felt very old. Twenty-eight, from where she sat, was old. She pulled up the flannel nightgown, inspected her belly. Bulging a little, not enough that they would tell. She stroked it, stroked the old stretch marks, remembering this time seven years ago when it was Kevin in there. They would both be September babies, Virgo. She wiped, and at least the toilet paper was soft. Not like in Scotland. Spiky hard stuff there, like cheap butcher-paper. At least America has soft toilet paper. She flushed the toilet. And good plumbing. Ian could have his damn Scotland, lucky for her she didn't marry him anyway. This would be an American baby, and the hell with Ian and his Beethoven quartets and stiff toilet paper, his abortion money. She'd lost one child already, well perhaps not lost. But she wanted this one. She glanced at the mirror again, old-looking.

Watch: 4:30. Harry wouldn't come for her for six hours. She flicked through the Gideon Bible, looking for names. It would be Seth if it was a boy. Girls names were harder. Naomi? Rachel? Dozed, flipping through the Bible looking for omens, advice, anything.

Four hours later she washed her hair, took a long shower, let the hot water beat on the base of her skull. Perfume after. Smell nice for Kevin. She remembered when she was little, living with Gran, and her Mama would come visit on weekends. Mama wore Taboo, and she had long, thick auburn hair. Carrie would watch Mama screw up her long hair into pin curls at night. Mama was very pretty. Mama had ridden on a float in a high school beauty parade, and her picture was on the mantle. Carrie looked at her own face, large-featured, plain; her hair, short, straight, brittle. Carrie was not very pretty, and she was sorry. She sprayed lots of perfume.

On the way to the house, Carrie tried to be pleasant, to make nice conversation.

"How's Gloria?"

"Aw, she's feelin pretty punk. Got her period. It's early. And a cold. We've both got colds." Harry hawked in his throat, spat out the window. Lit a Kent.

"Sorry to hear that." Carrie didn't give a shit.

"Got to stop an get doughnuts. She's not up to cookin this mornin."

"Is Kevin up?"

"Sure. Both the boys're watchin cartoons. We have a schedule around here. Cartoons on Saturday mornin, then they got their chores. Kevin feeds the cats an dogs, an John takes care 'a the horses."

"Horses?"

"Yep. Couple months back we got John a gelding. Got a little Shetland for Kevin. Got a place about fifteen miles out, six acres. We're gonna move next month, if we git all our gear packed by then."

Carrie smiled, sincere this time. "You're gonna be a shit-kicker yet, Harry. I guess you always had it in you."

"Yep," he leaned back from the steering wheel, tugged at his belt beneath his middle, "yep. I never cared much for cities. A boy needs space to grow in. Needs to learn responsibility. Needs a regular routine, rules. Fresh air."

She felt him accusing again. She lived in an apartment. In a city. She didn't know what a boy needs. Never could get dinner on the table the same time twice. That was how he got Kevvy away from her in the first place. She used to believe him. He used to accuse, and yes, she felt, yes, I'm guilty. I'm not good for him, not made to be a mother. Yes, she said, yes, a boy needs a father. A boy needs space. Rules. Yes. Crucify me. Now she was older, had been crucified enough.

Harry got his doughnuts, got Gloria a box of Kotex. Carrie went in with him and bought a carton of plain yogurt. She was hungry, her hands shook, damp. A little yogurt to settle the stomach. Back in the car, Harry droned on.

"I told the Corporation," again adjusting his belly, "told em I got the sales district I want, an they can just forget about any more promotions or transfers. I done had it with that ulcer factory in central office. The kind of work I do, I git bonuses bigger'n some of their salaries. I can milk this area for more than any district in the country, and I'm onna stay here." They drove into the suburbs, beyond the McDonalds stand, the Dairy Queen, several

213

used car lots and shopping centers, out San Pedro Boulevard into a sort of semi-country area of three and four acre plots. Castle Hills.

They pulled up to the front gate. Harry got out, flabbed over to the gate, untied the rope, shooed off Kevin's pony. He got in, pulled the car through. Got out again, roped the gate to, got in again. It was taking forever.

Carrie lifted her case full of presents out of the back seat, slung her purse and camera over her shoulder. Soon now, soon. It was heavy heartbeats again, pumping against her heart.

Kevin got up from the couch as she came in. He was so tall. Harry's face. He got Harry's face. But he wasn't fat, not yet, and he was gentle. He got her gentleness, she thought. And her intelligence. Heart beating against her throat, her waistband.

"Hi Kevin." She felt clumsy.

"Hi Cay-rie." Harry had said he must call her Carrie. He called Gloria Mama. Harry had said it would confuse him to have two Mamas.

"I brought presents," Carrie said. "I know it's after Christmas, but I couldn't come at Christmas, but I had all these presents. I tried to come sooner, but your daddy said I'd have to wait till this weekend." She collapsed with all her paraphernalia on the couch, began opening the case. Gloria's son John came in, quiet, and sat at the end of the couch. Carrie handed him a Beatles record. "Merry Christmas, John." He took it, rolling his eyes.

"Happy Easter more like it," he said. "It's March, y'know."

Gloria was standing in the doorway. "Whattaya say, John?"

"Thank you ma'am." John eased out of the room as quickly as he had come in.

"Kevin," Carrie felt breathless, "Kevvy, look." She lifted out a stack of boxes, most of them still in Christmas paper, a little faded now.

"What IS it?" His eyes were wide, his face all pink. "Lemme see!" For ages Kevvy unwrapped his presents: a tape player, eight cassette tapes, five books. "Neat-o. Yeah. Oh, Neat-o."

He was pleased. Carrie felt all golden. He was pleased, she'd done well. He thumbed through the Tall Book of Giant Stories, tapping his foot to the Beatles tape. She'd given him a tape of the same record she gave John, just to be sure there was no fighting over who got the best music. John's record player blared out from the bedroom, "Michelle, ma belle . . . . " She had done well.

Gloria stepped out of the doorway and flopped into her chair, lighting a Salem King. Kevin held up one of his new books to her. She nodded, smiled, saccharine. She looked at the television, soundless now beneath competing Beatles.

"Kevin, you pick up 'at paper all over the floor, you hear?" She ignored Carrie, who was picking up the paper and stuffing it in the tape player box. She was nervous, ill at ease in her own house, and Carrie was sorry it had to cost them all so much.

"I'm whipped already, and it ain't even eleven a clock," Gloria said as Harry came in and sat in his chair. "Had ta ahrn Kevin a shirt so he'd look nice."

Carrie wanted to say it wasn't necessary, wanted to say she wouldn't care if he were naked, would prefer him in a sweatshirt and cut-offs, anything. Their values were so different. Carrie didn't know what to say, felt she should apologize. Said nothing, smiled to the woman with platinum blonde hair who had waxed the floors in her honor, fearing and hating.

"Let's go to your room, OK Kevin?" Carrie wanted to run.

Gloria stopped them, "Boy, you git in 'air an git one a them doughnuts an drank some milk fore you run off."

Kevin didn't respond, started for the kitchen.

"What's at you said, boy?" Harry shouted.

"Yes ma'am."

"That's better."

Gloria added, "Don't you start forgittin your manners already and she ain't even been here a half hour."

Carrie swallowed. "Come on Kev. I've got some yogurt. We can both eat in the kitchen."

As they ate across from each other, forced conspirators, Carrie began to relax. Later, in his room, it was even better. Until Carrie noticed his empty bookcase.

"Kevin, what happened to all your books? All those books I've sent you? Last August the bookcase was nearly full!"

"Mom packed em up at Christmas," he said, his voice soft so no one would overhear.

"Why?"

"Dad said they make me lazy. I can get em back after we move to the new house." Kevin was sitting on the bed. He swung his leg so his heel dug into the floor. "Let's watch TV," he said, getting up to flick on the black and white set he'd inherited when the color set came for the living room. It was Popeye. Carrie sat on the floor by the bed, coloring in the Sendak coloring book she'd purchased so many months ago, before Christmas, when she was still going to marry Ian and move to Scotland.

Almost as though Kevin heard her thoughts, he said, "What happened to that guy you were gonna bring here at Christmas?"

"Oh. Well, he wasn't just a 'guy' Kevin. He was a very nice man. You would have liked him. A doctor. And he had his very own sailboat." Carrie knew Harry would have laughed at Ian. Harry thought all men who weren't Texans were faggots, especially Europeans, especially if they wore sandals. "See Kevin, like I told you on the phone, I was supposed to get married at Christmas."

"And go across the ocean."

"Yeah, where the castles are. And you would come visit me sometimes over there and see them. Except I didn't get married after all."

"Did the man go back to his home across the ocean?"

"Yes. You still have your globe? I could show you where it is."

"Nope. It's packed up too."

"Kevin, did they pack up everything I ever gave you?"

"Uh huh." He looked at Popeye again. Brutus was gripping him by the neck and bashing his head against a brick wall.

Gloria served lunch at 2:30, it being a weekend. Fried eggs, sausage, refrigerator biscuits, and a huge bowl of white cream gravy. Cokes. Carrie asked for a glass of milk, watched Gloria pour gravy over the boys' plates. "No gravy for me, please."

"You on a diet?" Gloria asked. It was the first time this trip that Gloria had spoken directly to her.

"Yes. Yes, I guess so," Carrie answered. She stared at the pools of grease on her eggs as Gloria passed a plate to her. She swallowed a mouthful of sausage and couldn't think of anything to say. She looked out the window at one of their sheep.

"That's the best lawnmower you can buy," Harry snapped, breaking the silence of clinking forks and knives.

Carrie jumped slightly. She hadn't realized he was watching her. But of course. Three years. He used to say he could read her like a book. She smiled at Kevin. Like hell, she thought. Like hell he could read her. He reduced everything to the sort of vulgar, thick, flabby cliche level he thought in. Kevin, on the other hand, Kevin had her mind. Labyrinthine, jagged in places, full of secret compartments opening on private islands. She had noticed the surface of Kevin's eyes go blank sometimes, had seen him leave these people as she would leave them, had seen him making his private journeys. Her son.

Kevin finished eating. "MayIPleaseBeExcused?"

"Yep." Harry answered.

Carrie got up to follow Kevin, smiling apology to Gloria. "Me too, I'm not very hungry."

Harry sneered, "You don't look like you're in good shape."

"I'm in better shape than you are," Carrie snapped, feeling childish and ill at the same time. Back in the bedroom she suggested to Kevin they take a walk.

"Outside the gate?" he asked.

"Sure, if they say it's OK."

"Oh boy, can we go to Hill Country Store and get an Icee?"

"Sure."

"Neat-o." He pulled on his cowboy boots.

Miraculously, she felt, Harry let them go. It was about a two-mile walk to the store and back. They found treasures in the grass: a feather, a dessicated turtle shell, an old boot. Together they made up a detective story, adding bits and pieces.

"And then they jumped in the car . . . "

"But it wouldn't start."

"So they started running, and . . . "

"The cops were chasin them . . . "

On the way back from the store, Kevin asked, "When can you come back again? Can you come at my birthday?"

"Before then I hope, Kev. I can't come at your birthday." She wanted to tell him, prepare him. She paused, then, "Cause of a secret."

"What? Come on, what's the secret?"

She ached to tell, but feared what Harry would do if he found out. Might not let her come again, might make this the last of the weekend visits. The divorce had only said she had "Weekend visitation at reasonable intervals, at the discretion of the child's father." That because she wasn't present to contest the divorce and had given up custody already.

"Are you gettin married and goin away?" he asked.

"No. Promise you won't tell, if I tell you?"

"Cross my heart and hope to die, stick a needle in my eye."

Carrie winced, then smiled. "Well," she dawdled with it, uncertain.

"Come on, come on," he pulled at her sleeve.

"Well, Kev, I have a little baby in my belly, and it's going to be born right around your birthday."

"Yeah? Really?" He looked at her belly, patted it. "But you're not fat. Aunt Sandy had a baby, but she had a fat, I mean a BIG fat belly first."

"Mine'll get big later on this summer," she said. "If I get to come see you in July, it'll be real big, and you can put your hand on it and feel it kick, just like you kicked when you were in there."

Kevin looked disbelieving. Then he giggled, slurped on his

Icee, kicked a rusty beer can. "Neat-o," he murmured, smiling. "How big is it now?"

"Just about this size," Carrie said, holding her thumb and index finger about an inch apart.

"Wow." Kevin said, "Neat-o."

"Don't tell anyone now, it's just our secret."

When Kevin asked to be excused after dinner, Harry told him to go take his bath.

"And git ready for bed," Gloria threw in. "Double quick. I'll come help ya wash it off."

While Gloria and Kevin were in the bathroom, Carrie watched TV with Gloria's eleven-year-old and Harry. They all kept silence. Later, Carrie couldn't remember what had been on. Her mind was in the bathroom with Kevin. She wiped her palms on the couch beside her, felt the tightness in her neck and shoulders. The bathroom door opened and Kevvy came out, dressed in pajamas.

"Kiss em goodnight, Kevin," Gloria ordered.

Kevin said, "John, you better go take your bath too," and his eyes gleamed as he came over and kissed first Carrie's cheek and then Harry's. John glared until Harry said,

"Go on, John."

Carrie asked Harry to take her back to the motel then. It was the night of the Grammy Awards, and Helen Reddy won, singing "I Am Woman," bra-less in a red dress in Carrie's spotless motel room.

When Harry brought her to the house Sunday morning, Kevin was in the back yard, his tape player at his side. That pleased her. She sat beside him on the ground where he was at work with a screwdriver, trying to dismantle a rusty powermower.

"I didn't mean to play that trick on you," he said. "Mom and daddy made me do it so they could get you to leave."

Something in Carrie grew very still, almost frozen. "What trick?"

"Me 'n John get to stay up till ten on Friday and Saturday nights. After you left I got up and we ate ice cream and watched TV."

Carrie felt dizzy. She leaned close to Kevin, touched his shoulder, held onto his upper arm. "Oh, Kev, that was an ugly thing for them to do." It wasn't a crying thing. It was an angry and yet an acid thing, eating her up, burning. They had ridiculed her. Had made him do it, had sat eating ice cream. Had made him participate in it, her own son. She clenched her teeth against a helpless rage, against this man with so much power. She watched Kevin work a screw loose in the mower.

Kevin murmured, "Don't think about it, OK? That's what I do. Just don't think about it."

Carrie touched his hair, tender and lost. "You sound very grown up, Kev." Then, sadly, "Before we stop thinking about it, do you understand why it hurts me?"

"Yeah," he said. "Just don't think about it. Let's go out front. You can watch me ride my bike faster than a thunderbird."

Out front she sat so she could lean against a tree and watched him ride his bike like a thunderbird, around and around the gravel drive that circled in front of their house. She hadn't eaten, and her head hurt. The anger was acid, eating her. She hummed "I Am Woman," whipping her mind for options, for possible action.

Gloria's John came out whittling a stick and whistling. He squatted by Carrie and stared at her for a minute. She smiled a little at him and asked, almost roughly,

"What's that?"

"Just a stick. Makin a point on it. You ain't married or nothin, are you?"

"No, I used to be married to Harry." Her voice grew flat.

"I mean now."

"No, I'm not married now." Under control again, kind again to this child who had nothing to do with. Indulgent.

"Well," he paused, "well how can you git pregnant if you ain't married?"

Karen held onto her sides, tight, her arms crossed in front. Sweat again, prickling around her hairline. "Kevin told you?"

"He told mama last night takin his bath. After daddy got back an she told him he got some mad. After, me 'n Kevin was wond'rin, cause mama told us before that women only git pregnant after they git married. Is Harry gonna be the daddy?"

"Oh God," Karen said, sitting on the ground and pressing against the tree. Her tone came out soft, weak, tired. "John, it's so much to explain. You get pregnant when you love someone very close, and it can happen if you're married or not. It's nothing bad. I'm very happy to have a baby growing inside me. And Harry certainly is not the daddy. It's —oh," she shook her head, helpless. "Sometimes it's too much to explain, John."

Harry startled them from behind the tree. "It's not enough you gotta get Kevin upset, you think you can turn my whole family upside down, do you? Get them all confused."

Kevin threw down his bike and came over.

"Carrie," Harry said, stepping on a cigarette butt and grinding it under his foot, "I reckon it's time you were leavin."

"But my bus isn't till 7:45 tonight. It's not even lunch yet."

"Well, there's a change of plans. When I picked you up this morning I didn't know you'd have the nerve to go tryin to justify yourself to John, here. I don't want my boys exposed to this kind of thing. You're goin now."

Kevin stared at his shoes. John whittled a point on his stick, and inside the house Gloria banged noisily in the kitchen window. Harry spoke again, calm, flat-voiced as though he were commenting on the weather.

"I reckon I can call the police if I have to. You're on my property."

Kevin snapped his head up at Harry. "How come, Daddy?"

"Go on in the house, boy." Harry answered. John whittled off and Kevin started to move.

"Wait a minute," Carrie said, standing up and brushing off. "Kevin, wait. I'm going, but I'll be back, and maybe we'll fix it so you can come visit me at my house, and not just for a weekend, either. Just let me kiss you goodbye for now, OK?" Kevin looked at his father. Harry didn't move. Carrie took Kevin's face in both damp hands and kissed him, briefly.

It was long to the bus station, and Carrie seethed, silent. Hatred like vomit welled in her throat as Harry drove her through San Antonio, and she didn't say. Harry sat nervous, tried to whistle, drummed his fingers on the door frame. Finally Carrie said,

"I'm getting a lawyer."

"Good luck, you with your illegitimate kid. You'll look great in court in a few months."

"Yes I will," she said. "Yes, I surely will." She knew how she would look. She would call Legal Aid from the bus

station, go over for an interview today. The bus wasn't
for seven hours.

Harry lit a cigarette and curled his lips into a sneer.
"Yep. I can read you like a book. You don't scare me.
You'll go runnin back to your artsy-craftsy graduate school
friends. Professional students, bunch of commies and
queers the lot of you. Put all of you together you wouldn't
have the price of a lawyer in five years."

He pulled up in front of the bus station. Carrie got out,
hefted her worn white bag out of the back seat in an arc
to the sidewalk, and kicked the car door shut so hard it
rattled the chassis. If I have to, she thought, I can do anything. She stormed the bus station, square-shouldered,
pregnant, and ready.